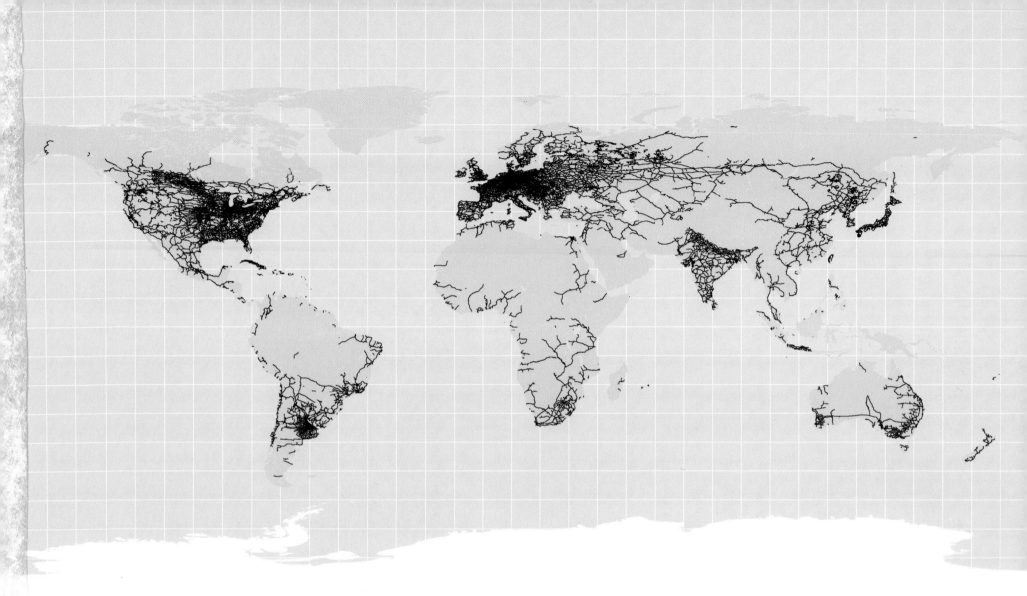

RAILWAY MAPS OF THE WORLD

We live on a planet that has at one time or another been covered in *four million* kilometers of rail track. The map above, first published in the *New Scientist* magazine in 2008, shows the relative position of all current lines.

VIKING

Published by the Penguin Group

Penguin Group (USA) Inc., 375 Hudson Street, New York, New York 10014, U.S.A. · Penguin Group (Canada),
90 Eglinton Avenue East, Suite 700, Toronto, Ontario, Canada M4P 2Y3 (a division of Pearson Penguin Canada
Inc.) · Penguin Books Ltd, 80 Strand, London WC2R 0RL, England · Penguin Ireland, 25 St. Stephen's Green,
Dublin 2, Ireland (a division of Penguin Books Ltd) · Penguin Books Australia Ltd, 250 Camberwell Road,
Camberwell, Victoria 3124, Australia (a division of Pearson Australia Group Pty Ltd) · Penguin Books India
Pvt Ltd, 11 Community Centre, Panchsheel Park, New Delhi – 110 017, India · Penguin Group (NZ),
67 Apollo Drive, Rosedale, Auckland 0632, New Zealand (a division of Pearson New Zealand Ltd) ·
Penguin Books (South Africa) (Pty) Ltd, 24 Sturdee Avenue, Rosebank, Johannesburg 2196, South Africa

Penguin Books Ltd, Registered Offices: 80 Strand, London WC2R 0RL, England

First published in 2011 by Viking Penguin, a member of Penguin Group (USA) Inc.

10 9 8 7 6 5 4 3 2 1

Copyright © Mark Ovenden, 2011   All rights reserved

Illustration credits appear on page 135.

ISBN 978-0-670-02265-6

Printed in the United States of America

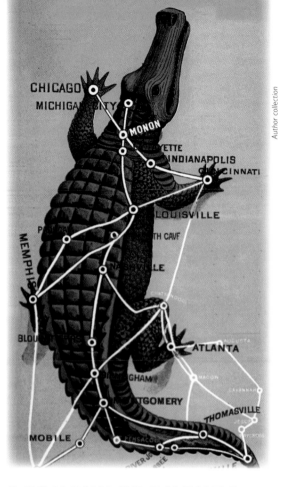

Author collection

RAILWAY MAPS OF THE WORLD

www.railwaymapsoftheworld.com

www.markovenden.com

*While gathering material for this book, every attempt has been made to contact copyright owners; where this has
not been possible, we extend our apologies and thank them for their contribution to this history.*

Most images have been reproduced with the kind permission of rail operators, the Library of Congress,
Washington, D.C., the National Railway Museum, York, England, or from private collectors who have
cherished and preserved them for years and to whom the author and publisher extend their gratitude.

Front jacket art with thanks to:
Kim Ji-hwan (top), California State Railroad Museum, Marc H. Choko, Library of Congress (bottom row).
Title page world rail map with thanks to: European Union Joint Research Centre / Tim Makins
Layout by author with assistance from Lucy and Ivan Frontani
Typeset in Gill Sans Light with Regular, Bold, Light, and Italic headlines

ACKNOWLEDGMENTS

This book would not have been possible without the kind help
and valued support of:

*ADEMAS, Kerry D'Agostino, Jean-Pierre Arnault, Mike Ashworth,
Alan Baillie, Jöel Bedos, Jury Bondarau, Chris Brownbill, Jean-Patrick
Charrey, Pat Chessell, Marc H. Choko, Patrick Clancey, Tom and Elaine
Colchie, Beverley Cole, Mike Cooper-Difrancia, Jennie Doble, Andrew
Dow, Reinhard Drechsler, Geoff Edwards, John Edwards, David Ellis,
Jeff Ferzoco, Yonah Freemark, Lucy and Ivan Frontani, Arun Ganesh,
Roman Hackelsberger, Paul Holroyd, Maria Holubowicz, Valerie
Hutchinson, Mecca Ibrahim, Eddie Jabbour, Kim Ji-hwan, Deborah Jones,
Dr. James A. Jones, Michael Kerins, Struan Kerr, George and Sue King,
Eva-Lotta Lamb, Martin Langley, La Vie Du Rail, Barry Lawrence, David
Lawrence, Peter Lloyd, Bernard Lohmöller, John McCarthy, Malcolm
McCrow, Alistair Meek, Rudi Meyer, Brenda and Neil Northfield, Julian
Pepinster, Pascal Pontremoli, Lucas Quispe, Maxwell J. Roberts, Mike
Rohde, David Rumsey, Simon Sadler, Christopher Saynor, John Saxton,
Robert Schwandl, Robert Shepherd, Dr. Guy Slatcher, Andrew Smithers,
Giorgio Stagni, Jan Suchy, John Thomason, Richard Thorogood, Darren
Tossell, Maggie Turner, Massimo Vignelli, Julie Vion-Broussailles, Mike
Walton, Andrew Williams, Christian Wolmar, Robin Woods, Julian
Worricker, Kyle Wyatt, Alan Yearsley, Bill Yenn, Dmitry Zinoviev.*

CONTENTS

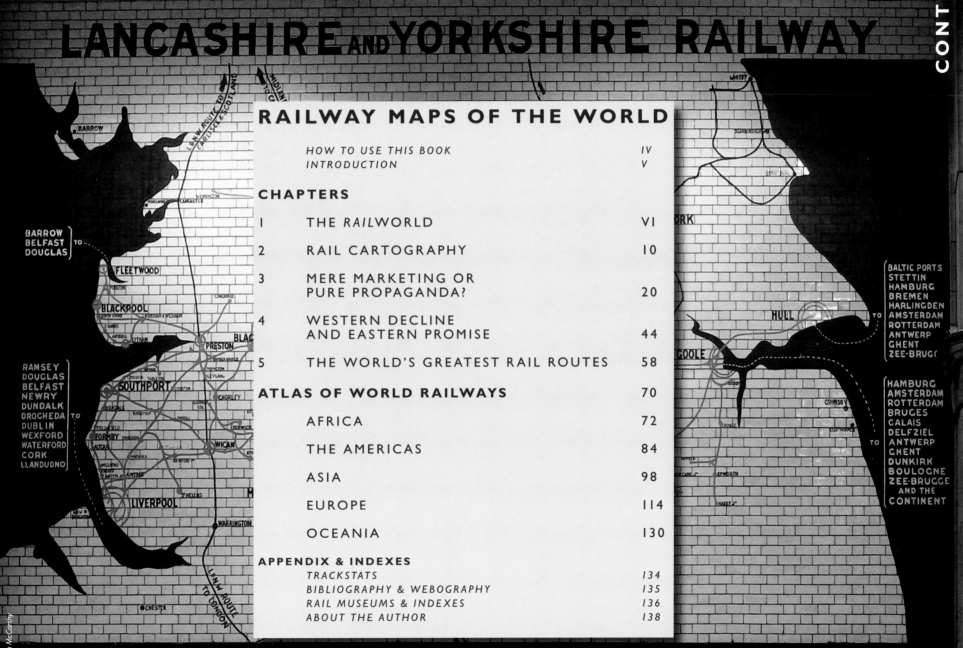

RAILWAY MAPS OF THE WORLD

John McCarthy

How to use this book

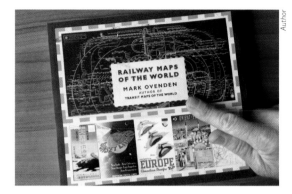

There are several methods that could have been employed to present this collection of maps: a simple chronological progression starting with surveys of Britain's pioneering 1820s lines and ending with photographs of the latest online "moving" train maps. Or it could have been laid out as a geographical breakdown, maybe simply A–Z by country or continent. The collection could also have been broken down by style—engineers maps, platform diagrams, timetable info, posters, pocket guides, etcetera.

As is often the case in such an endeavor, the most obvious way often does not prevail. In the course of research, major variations in style, quality, and quantity of maps produced was unearthed: certain countries have produced enough maps and posters to fill several books of their own, and selecting which to include led to some tough choices. In other countries—despite lots of rail lines—it seems little or no printed mapping has ever existed, hence the choice is limited (Eritrea, for example). More than just a map issue, some relatively large countries like Greenland, Chad, and Yemen simply have no rail tracks at all. Other quite small countries—the Benelux, for example—are crisscrossed by thousands of lines. A purely geographical approach would have inevitably resulted in some countries being underrepresented or others having insufficient space. Another editorial decision was needed over the sheer quantity. As railways are not just used for moving passengers—in fact they were first used for transporting heavy materials, and still perform that task efficiently today—it would be impossible in one book (and possibly a little dull for the reader!) to show a map of every existence of metal rails on the planet.

The mass of material produced throughout history raises the possibility of presenting it in a purely chronological manner. Despite their seemingly enduring appearance (rail track is often called "permanent way"), railroads are constantly constructed, disassembled, and rebuilt. Counting everything from quarries and dockyards, horse-drawn streetcars and subways, mountain railways and funiculars,

transcontinental thoroughfares and heritage steam lines to the latest high-speed rail routes, there may have been as many as four million kilometers of tracks laid at different times over the entire planet. Following a thirty-year period after World War II (when tracks were ripped up all over the globe) there are now just over one million, but with hundreds of kilometers of new high-speed lines recently opened and thousands more planned, the cumulative total is rising again.

A chronological look would never have been exhaustive in 144 pages, not to mention that this would have morphed into a history lesson rather than a celebration of beautiful maps! The author has attempted in this and his previous books to pay homage to style and aesthetics, with special attention to how a map's appearance speaks to the unique concerns of presenting the rails—the blending of geography, marketing, design, and readability. So in the spirit of displaying the widest range of styles, and being practical yet relatively comprehensive, this book is laid out in a hybrid approach:

The first five *chapters* (pages VI–69) are chronological inasmuch as they cover the evolution of railroads from the Liverpool and Manchester Railway of 1830 to the proposed high-speed networks of China in the 2020s. But inevitably within each chapter there are some more recent maps compared alongside older ones. This affords the opportunity for contrasting peak service provision with current levels, for example pages 46–57.

The *atlas* section (pages 70–133) is purely alphabetical by the English spelling of continent, then country name. Here invariably the most recent example of the official contemporary passenger service map is provided, where available. Historical maps are occasionally also shown to contrast that country's progression (or regression). There is more space allocated to countries that have produced more maps. In the cases of the most prolific—India, for example—it is clearly not possible to show maps from every line or operator, so some editorial discretion has been employed (this does not imply that any one service or company is better

than one not included). Some countries that have recently closed their services *are* shown (Botswana, Liberia, Ecuador, for example), and some that are being built or planned (Libya) have been put in the atlas, but countries that have not had any rail services for many years are not included (Barbados, Cyprus, Lebanon, Cambodia, etc).

Given the sheer number of railroads and styles, operating companies and uses, it is clear that this book cannot possibly include every rail map ever produced, though many excellent additional examples are shown on the accompanying Web site, www.railwaymapsoftheworld.com, and the resource guides on page 135 will unlock further delights. These then are the guiding editorial principles of *Railway Maps of the World*:

* At least one map from each country where passenger rail services are operating.

* At least one example of each cartographic style, from the most basic signal box diagrams to the most detailed panoramic works.

* A selected representation of the variety produced by the most prolific countries (Canada, France, UK, USA, Russia).

* Only official maps produced by the railroad operator.

* A focus on heavy-rail/main line/commuter/suburban passenger rail services (for subway and metro maps, consult *Transit Maps of the World*: see Bibliography, page 135).

* A bias toward maps that have aesthetic appeal!

In any collection of historical material, allowances should be made for quality. Though huge efforts have been made to find high-resolution maps from every country currently operating passenger railroads, where this has not been possible the author begs forgiveness for the handful of somewhat lower-quality maps that have been permitted to be consistent with the editorial guidelines. In addition, with such a wide field, there will be omissions, so do please get in touch if there are any suggestions for inclusion in future editions. Lastly, it is hoped the reader will indulge the author a few strays from the self-imposed guidelines, simply because some of the maps presented here were too good to leave out!

Rail tracks put places *"on the map"*

CENTER: Detail from an 1897 map of the Missouri-Kansas-Texas (often known as the "Katy") Railroad, which had built many kilometers of lines into sparsely populated areas after Congress promised land grants to the first railroad to reach the Kansas border. The land, however, remained Indian Territory after a court battle.

LOWER RIGHT: Cover of a 1922 Southern Pacific brochure encouraging settlers to the wide-open spaces of the then relatively empty state of California.

Many railroads were deliberately built "in the middle of nowhere" or serving what, on the face of it, would be unprofitable communities, with the deliberate and sole intent that immigrants would come and make the rail company's investment worthwhile. They often did!

We think nothing in the twenty-first century of racing hundreds if not thousands of kilometers in a few short hours: traversing states, countries, even entire hemispheres. But before the railways, communication over anything farther than walking distance necessitated a Herculean effort. The fastest any one person could travel was on horseback; "roads" such as they were, were little more than dirt tracks. Moving several people at once, or transporting any kind of heavy material, was a mission requiring much time, considerable determination, and usually a large financial investment.

In 1800, less than a billion people stood on planet Earth. Just four generations later, when the railways reached their peak in the early 1920s, that figure had doubled. It had previously taken almost half a millennium for the population to increase by that proportion. Though other factors were of course at work (not the least of which were major improvements in health and nutrition), most scholars cite the railways as crucial, if not key, to the exponential economic booms of the Industrial Revolution and the dawning of the modern age.

Those booms increased not only population, but urban areas in particular. Settlements had been established piecemeal, over millennia, predominantly along coasts or inland waterways, or at least where horses, camels, or elephants could easily navigate.

The interiors of the great continents before the railways were almost completely unpopulated, save for small isolated pockets. The advent of the steam engine and the railroad locomotive in the nineteenth century would significantly alter that. As early as the 1700s, short permanent routes of long iron rails began to prove themselves as potentially useful thoroughfares on which to move large, bulky materials (coal, especially), albeit still rather laboriously. A handful of wise thinkers began contemplating what might be possible if steam-powered machines were able to drag behind them bigger and heavier loads, including carrying people relatively quickly over longer distances.

One of the first of these was Englishman William James, who as early as 1815 had proposed laying iron tracks between the naval yards at Portsmouth and Chatham (127 km). In 1822 he surveyed a route between Liverpool Docks and central Manchester, sending out engineers to explore the topography and the dangerous marshy terrain called Chat Moss. Most vital to James's endeavor was a detailed map of the area; but none was available. So was born the earliest mapping for the purpose of crossing land on a railway.

Surveyors across Europe and America were soon miles from home—the diggers, navvies, and tracklayers were out in open country, without much shelter, sanitation, or even a bar!

Those early railway pioneers therefore found themselves needing encampments, which expanded into tiny settlements servicing them, which in turn grew into villages and towns. Eventually, some would grow into great metropolises. The era of inland cities had dawned and urbanization became inextricably linked with railroads—this was how remote places quite literally got put "on the map."

ABOVE: As the name suggests on this 1950s station "totem" sign from West Sussex, England, this once tiny fishing port was not much more than a village before the advent of mass railroad travel. But once the Brighton to Portsmouth line arrived in 1863, fortunes changed and holidaymakers flocked. By the 1920s it was being promoted as "The Children's Paradise" and is now home to the world headquarters of The Body Shop and part of Britain's twelfth largest conurbation (Brighton/Hove/Worthing/Littlehampton, population: 461,181).

THE *RAILWORLD*

BACKGROUND: Drifting furtively over
the Earth, thousands of man-made
satellites peer down continuously at
the glowing electric filaments of light
flowing along invisible chords. From up
here it seems hard to imagine what
might link these isolated clusters of
energy-burning beacons or why they
follow such regimented, almost straight
lines. By daylight an informed observer
might guess the layout is due to the
wide flat concrete rivers we call roads.
But the truth is that almost the entire
pattern of human settlement creeping
across the great continents of America,
Asia, and Australasia owes its location
and growth to another form of land
transportation: the railways.

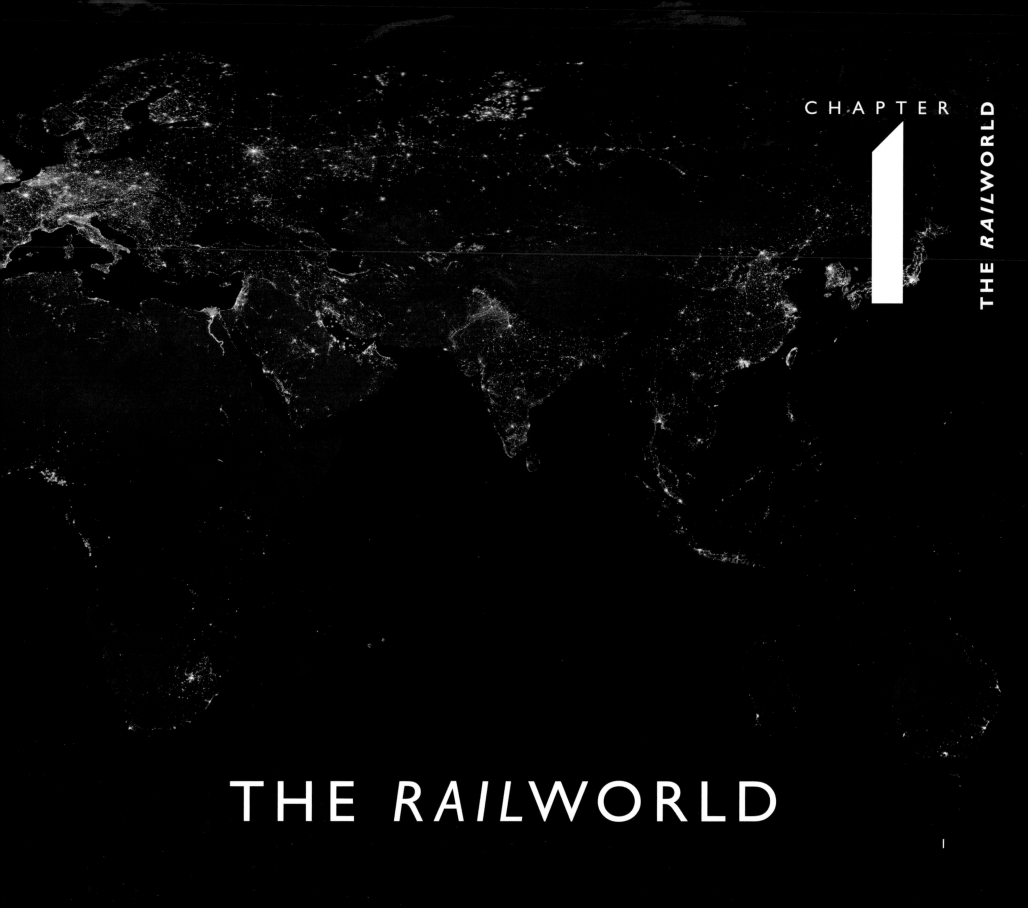

THE *RAILWORLD*

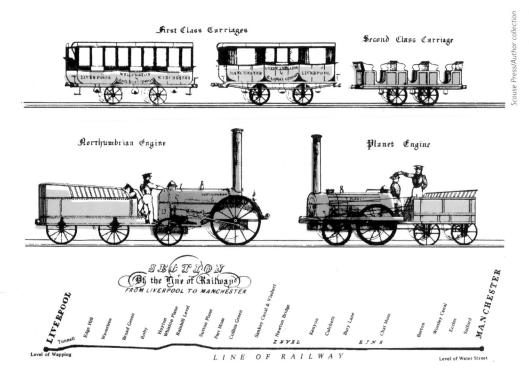

First Class Carriages

Second Class Carriage

Northumbrian Engine

Planet Engine

SECTION
Of the Line of Railway
FROM LIVERPOOL TO MANCHESTER

LIVERPOOL — Tunnell — Level of Wapping — Edge Hill — Wavertree — Broad Green — Roby — Huyton — Whiston Plane — Rainhill Level — Sutton Plane — Parr Moss — Collins Green — Sankey Canal & Viaduct — Newton Bridge — Kenyon — Culcheth — Bury Lane — Chat Moss — Barton — Worsley Canal — Eccles — Salford — MANCHESTER — Level of Water Street

LEVEL LINE

LINE OF RAILWAY

While the predecessors of a guide "track" concept can be traced back as early as Greco-Roman times, and though many eighteenth-century mines and quarries were experimenting with wagons on permanent rights of way, the world's first railroads as we would recognize them were built in Europe and America from the early 1800s onwards.

In Britain, the rails brought fresh sea fish to the rapidly industrializing cities—nourishing paupers in the "dark satanic mills" and giving birth to the staple diet of the English: fish and chips. Wealthy professionals bought property on the edges of cramped and dirty places like Birmingham, Dublin, London, and Manchester and, thanks to the new train stations, could quickly travel to work in the city—effectively becoming the world's first commuters.

The most remote outposts of continental North America found themselves suddenly connected to the outside world. Railroads brought farm produce to the populated cities across the country, and spurred development in America's Midwest, where entire networks of rail tracks were laid to serve vast new farming regions. Railroad companies acted as realtors, selling off large lots of "untouched" land to prospective farmers (usually with scant regard for indigenous people). Geographers, historians, and economists agree that it was the railroad that not only opened up the interior of America and connected the industrialized eastern seaboard with the mineral-rich Pacific coast, but was the driving force of the economy for most of the nineteenth century.

LEFT: Contemporary illustration (circa 1830) of Robert Stephenson's engines, including a cartographic representation of the heights of the line; this is probably the earliest schematic of any railroad.
FACING LEFT: A handbill representing one of the earliest known pieces of railroad publicity, and the first known printed passenger rail timetable. Made in 1830 by the Liverpool and Manchester Railway.
FACING RIGHT: 1826 Survey of what became the world's first passenger line.
BELOW: 1827 technical drawing of the Stockton and Darlington railway route.

GNU

THE WORLD'S FIRST RAILWAYS

Precursors to the modern railway age. Those listed are firsts in their country or field or contributed to the evolution of railways (lists are not exhaustive, and do not include the innumerable small lines).

The double-tracked regular interurban steam-powered locomotive passenger service of England's Liverpool and Manchester Railway (1830, facing page), validated the viability of rail transit and started a construction boom—known in the 1840s as "Railwaymania"—that spread across the then developed world, ushering in the "Railway Age."

YEAR	COUNTRY	NAME	KILOMETERS		YEAR	COUNTRY	NAME	KILOMETERS
600BC	Greece	Isthmus of Corinth, Diolkos "Rutway" for moving ships over land	6–8		1830	England	Liverpool and Manchester Railway, regular steam passenger service	49.8
1550 circa	Germany	Hand-propelled mine tubs called "hunds"	—		1830	USA	Baltimore & Ohio Railway, steam operations	41.8
1604	England	Wollaton Wagonway, first overland horse-drawn freight line	3.2		1831	England	Warrington and Newton Railway	7.2
1758	England	Middleton Railway, freight	1.6		1831	USA	Mohawk & Hudson Railroad	25.7
1803	Wales	Carmarthenshire Tram road	.6		1833	USA	South Carolina Canal and Rail Road Company	219
1803	England	Surrey Iron Road, first "public" railway	14.4		1834	Germany	Bavarian Ludwigsbahn (Nuremberg–Fürth)	7.2
1804	Wales	Penydarren Tram road, steam-hauled freight	3.2		1834	Ireland	Dublin and Kingstown Railway	9.6
1807	Wales	Oystermouth Railway, horse-drawn passenger line	6.4		1835	Belgium	Brussels–Mechelen	19.3
1808	England	Richard Trevithick's circular steam railway, London	—		1836	Canada	La Prairie–Saint-Jean-sur-Richelieu	25.7
1810	USA	Leiper Railroad, Pennsylvania	.1		1836	England	London and Greenwich Railway	3
1812	Scotland	Kilmarnock and Troon Railway	15.2		1837	Cuba	Havana–Bejucal	22.5
1812	England	Middleton Railway, commercial steam-hauled freight line	1.6		1837	Germany	Leipzig–Dresden Railway (Althen)	10
1825	England	Stockton and Darlington Railway, freight and passengers	41.8		1837	England	Grand Junction Railway	132
1827	Germany	Ceské Budéjovice and Leopoldschlag, horse-drawn	54.7		1837	Austria	Vienna–Wagram	13.7
1828	England	Bolton and Leigh Railway, steam freight	12		1837	Russia	Tsarskoye Selo–Saint Petersburg	24.1
1828	France	Saint-Etienne and Andrézieux, horse-drawn freight	23.3		1837	France	Paris Embarcadero–Le Pecq	18.2
1830	England	Canterbury and Whitstable Railway, steam cable-drawn	8		1839	Italy	Naples–Portici	7.2
1830	USA	Baltimore & Ohio Railway, horse-drawn	20.9		1839	Holland	Amsterdam–Haarlem	14.4

Travelling
BY THE
RAILWAY.

THE DIRECTORS of the LIVERPOOL and MANCHESTER RAILWAY beg leave to inform the Public, that on and after MONDAY next the 4th of October, the Railway Coaches will start from the Stations in Liverpool and Manchester respectively, at the following hours:—

The FIRST CLASS COACHES, Fare 7s.
At Seven o'Clock.
Ten o'Clock.
One o'Clock.
Half-past Four o'Clock.

The SECOND CLASS COACHES, Fare 4s.
At Eight o'Clock.
Two o'clock.

On Sundays, the First Class Coaches will start at Seven o'Clock in the Morning, and half-past Four in the Afternoon; and the Second Class Coaches at half-past Six in the Morning, and Four in the Afternoon.

Places may be booked at the Liverpool end, either at the Station in Crown-street, or at the Company's Coach Office, in Dale-street; and at the Manchester end at the Coach Office in Liverpool-road, or at the Company's Coach Office in Market-street, corner of New Cannon-street, where Plans of the Coaches constituting each Train will lie, in order that Passengers may make choice of their respective Seats. Tickets for which will be given on payment of the Fare.

A conveyance by Omnibuses twenty minutes before each of the above-mentioned hours of departure of the First Class Coaches only, will proceed from the Company's Office, Dale-street, to Crown-street, free of charge, for Sixty-eight Passengers and their Luggage, (the said number, first booked, having the preference, on their claiming it at the time of booking) and for the same number from Crown-street to Dale-street, on the arrival of the Coaches from Manchester, a preference on the same terms being given to Passengers first booked at the Company's Coach Offices, Manchester.

After the Festival week, during which it is impossible to ensure the desired accommodation, a conveyance to and from Crown-street will be provided for all the Passengers carried by the First Class Coaches.

Parcels will be received at any of the Company's Coach Offices, and delivered with the greatest regularity at the usual rates, and without any charge for booking or delivering.

No fee or gratuity is allowed to be taken by any Porter, Guard, Engine-man, or other servant of the Company, and the Directors are determined to enforce this regulation by the immediate dismissal of any person in their employ offending against it.

Railway Office, John-street, Liverpool, 30th September, 1830.

PRINTED BY BANCKS AND CO. EXCHANGE-STREET.

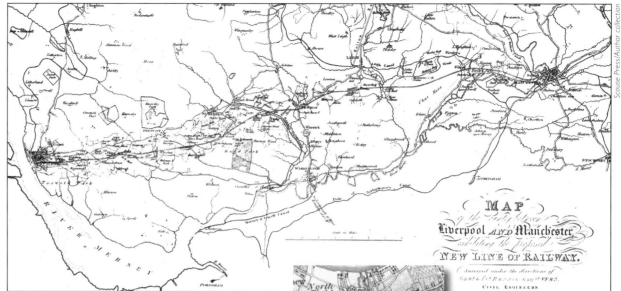

By the end of the 1830s Belgium, Britain, Canada, France, Germany, Ireland, Italy, and Russia had adopted the new technology. Many European colonies were, in turn, laid with track: Cuba as early as 1837, Jamaica 1845, Guyana 1848, Mexico 1850, Peru and Chile 1851, India and Pakistan in 1853, Australia, Egypt, and Brazil by 1854, and South Africa by 1860.

LEFT: London's Surrey Iron Road in 1816: arguably the first time a railway was ever depicted on a public map. BELOW: The Liverpool and Manchester shown on an 1829 map: "railroad" is not a term in common British usage!

The "Railway Age" begins… in Lancashire, England

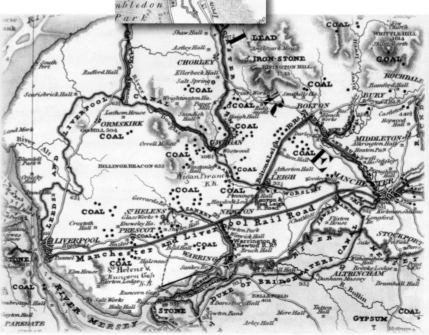

The Industrial Revolution was concentrated where resources—coal, water, investment wealth, and vast amounts of cheap labor—came together. In Britain, conditions were ideal in Lancashire, home to the world's then busiest port, Liverpool. Located in the far west of the county, Liverpool imported raw material for manufacture in booming Manchester—located at Lancashire's eastern end. Fifty kilometers of dangerous and bumpy road connected the two, and while canals sped up the transport of materials, wealthy merchants wanted faster shipping. Motivated by the large profits being made by canal owners, Henry Booth formed the Liverpool and Manchester Railway Company in May, 1823.

Several routes were examined, but eventually a 56 km line between the two metropolises was chosen by engineers George and John Rennie. The route, surveyed by Charles Blacker Vignole, required remarkable civil engineering feats for the age: a massive 2,057 m tunnel (the world's first underneath an existing city), a 3.2 km cutting through rock, a nine-arch viaduct, and a 7.6 km crossing of a notorious marshy bog. But what really gave the double-tracked line the edge was the choice of a steam-driven locomotive, now technologically capable of the immense task. The Liverpool and Manchester has an impressive list of firsts, and its gauge, signaling, locomotives, engineering, stations, timetables, and maps were emulated by new railways opening across England and the eastern United States. While improvements chugged on, the line is generally accepted as setting the standard in modern interurban passenger rail transport: the genuine railway godfather.

FRANCE FIRST BUT FALTERS

In France, as in Britain, the crucible of industrial growth was not in the lofty enlightened capital, but the gritty industrial coalfields, mostly around the Massif Central region. In 1823, the newly reinstated king, Louis XVIII, approved the building of the first French public *chemin de fer* (literally: iron way) between mines near Saint-Etienne and Andrézieux, a small town on the river Loire. Coal was to be transferred to boats for the long journey to Paris and northern France.

The single-track line took three years to get up and running, and even by then the locomotives were not ready, so wagons had to be pulled by horses. In 1832, after the introduction of steam, the line was extended into the city of Lyon; the 59-km-long route quickly became a more practical and popular means of transportation than the dreadful roads.

Apart from this and a lone steam tramway, the pace of development in France was halting, partly due to war. The next major line didn't open for almost a decade, by which time there had been significant advances in America, Germany, Belgium, and elsewhere.

Eventually, in 1837, a route from the edge of Paris to the royal estates around Le Pecq and Saint-Germain-en-Laye was built, and is cited as the country's first dedicated passenger service.

Adopting what was fast becoming the "standard" gauge of 1,435 mm, the Le Pecq line remained isolated from other small lines until the 1840s when France began serious construction of a full national network. By that time the much smaller British Isles had over 3,000 km of track, and it was possible to cross Germany from the Channel to modern-day Poland!

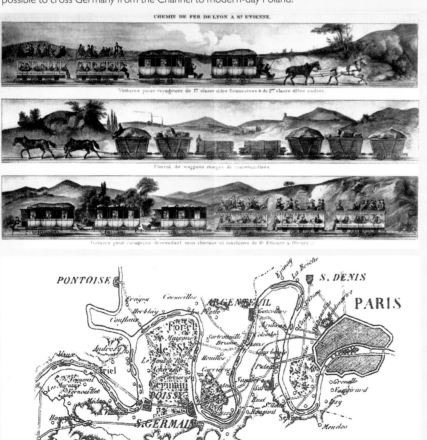

La Société d'Histoire du Vésinet collection

Jean Falaize collection

CANALS VERSUS TRAINS IN EASTERN USA

Eastern cities in the United States of America during the late eighteenth and early nineteenth centuries were like nothing that had come before them. With vast amounts of space to expand into, there was no need to squash new developments into existing ancient cities, as had so often been the case in Europe. Street layouts of these virgin cities—often with wide straight roads—enabled railways when they arrived to be reasonably easily accommodated.

Baltimore, Boston, Charleston, and Philadelphia were vying for supremacy, but New York had the most significant water-based connections in its massive harbor and the Erie Canal. In an attempt to keep apace, merchants in Philadelphia proposed an extravagant 555 km canal to link the city to the Ohio River. This limited aquatic outlook meant that the first rails in the eastern US would not come from either of the nation's two largest cities.

It was the investors of Baltimore (by 1830 the third largest city in the country)—with their hopes pinned on pushing into the interior and being able to link directly to the Midwest—who would pioneer major railway building. On July 4, 1828, the Baltimore & Ohio Railway Company dredged up the last surviving signatory to the Declaration of Independence, ninety-year-old Charles Carroll, to lay the first stone. Carroll is oft quoted as having felt his role in rail history even more significant than signing the 1776 document. The first 21 km to Ellicott Mills were ready by 1830. However, it was a branch to Washington, D.C., that preceded the original intention of getting to the Ohio River, which was not fully realized until 1852.

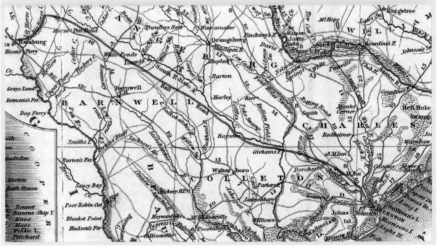

Library of Congress

Entire empires were born and made on the iron road. Having a railway nearby would soon prove to be a huge boost to virtually any hamlet, town, or city. When the Stockton and Darlington Railway, for example, was extended to the tiny cluster of houses by the sea at Middlesbrough, England, in 1833, few could have foreseen that its arrival would grow the population from 400 to 6,000 in just seven years, and that it would become a major port and, temporarily at least, the largest iron-making center in the world.

Such expansion at the cause of the railway was to be repeated across the globe wherever the tracks arrived, so much so that almost the entire pattern of human settlement was altered by the railways, at least for the first century or so of their existence.

ABOVE: Detail from a South Carolina Canal and Railroad 1833 map of their line between Charleston and Hamburg. CENTER LEFT: Vehicles on the Saint-Etienne to Lyon line, circa 1832. LOWER LEFT: 1844 sketch map of the Paris–Le Pecq line.

UPPER CENTER: The Baltimore & Ohio Railroad (shown in 1860) was a far greater endeavor than anything attempted in Europe when it started construction in 1828. Before it got to its intended destination on the Ohio (1852), it opened a branch to Washington, D.C., but quickly pushed through to Chicago and St. Louis, becoming one of the country's most important east-west systems.

While railways were establishing themselves piecemeal in the UK, US, and Europe, it was not immediately obvious that they would form interconnected networks.

The building of canals and waterways linking navigable rivers continued as if their reign would never end. In the decade following the opening of the Liverpool and Manchester railway, more kilometers of canal were completed than railroads. Although super-canals like the Suez and Panama were still to prove their worth, the days of smaller waterways as viable thoroughfares for heavy goods were numbered.

The 1840s saw an unprecedented rail construction boom. By 1850 tiny Britain had some 8,000 km of track. Around 3,000 km had been built in (what became) Germany by the same date, and the United States went from having less than 4,500 km of track in 1840 to 13,800 km by 1850.

Another country early to enthusiastically embrace rail was Belgium. A newly formed state in 1830, it saw an opportunity to bond north and south with the new technology, and unlike Britain and the USA, where private companies had been allowed to build their lines pretty much wherever they fancied (even duplicating routes and placing competing stations in the same town or city), Belgium began a governmental effort to build an interconnected nationwide railroad network.

The first section of line opened in 1835 between Brussels and Mechelen, and within five years the country had a perfect cross-shaped north-south/east-west start to what became one of the most dense rail systems—and the first nationalized one—in the world. The railway town of Mechelen had a grim role during the Nazi occupation as the site of a transit camp to deport Jews.

ABOVE: What appears today as a familiar satellite view of the Great Lakes and the vast plains of the American Midwest understates the immensity of the task facing early railroad builders. Before construction of the Baltimore & Ohio and other pioneering lines, the moving of goods and people by toll roads and waterways was slow and dangerous. The land had to be methodically surveyed before railroads could be built to open up the interior of the continent.

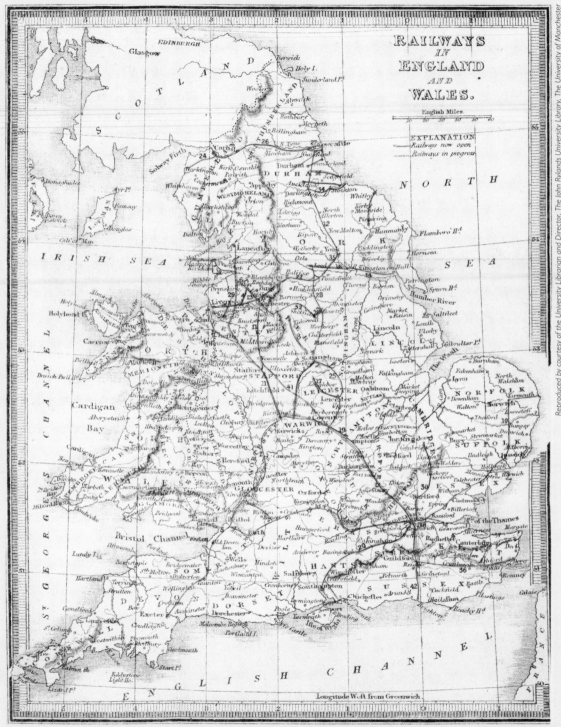

FIRST NATIONAL TIMETABLE AND MAP

In order to make a long journey on the newly opened British railway lines it was necessary to visit the station Booking Office to consult a dizzying array of timetables—from the many competing companies—at least a day in advance, before a ticket could even be bought!

Lancastrian George Bradshaw (1801) witnessed the building of the Liverpool and Manchester Railway, and professionally (as an engraver of canal maps) traveled much of the country on the rapidly expanded rail tracks across Britain. He eventually amassed the timetables of every company, and with great foresight created *Bradshaw's Railway Time Tables and Assistant to Railway Travelling* in 1839. It contained the world's first national rail system map and the first country-wide collection of train times, and was published as a waistcoat-pocket-sized guide.

The timetables and accompanying map needed regular updating as new lines and extensions marched across the countryside. *Bradshaw's Railway Manual* as it was renamed, expanded to include notes on each location served. *Bradshaw's* is oft quoted by literary characters such as Sherlock Holmes and its observations now offer a unique perspective on Victorian Britain. International editions covering first Continental Europe appeared from 1847, cementing the family name with effective travel, and making Bradshaw's guides world renowned—though George himself died in 1853.

ABOVE: Railroads were soon depicted in art. J. M. W. Turner's "Rain, Steam and Speed", first exhibited at the Royal Academy in 1844, believed to be a view toward London from the Maidenhead Rail Bridge (Brunel, 1838) between Taplow and Maidenhead, now hangs in the National Gallery, London.
CENTER: A "handy" guide for calculating local time in each North American city. Dating from the 1860s, it has Washington, D.C., at its center.
TOP LEFT: Station clock and signage at Uxbridge, West London.
CENTER LEFT: William Allen's 1883 standard railway time plan.
FACING FAR LEFT: Richard Evans 1841 portrait of George Bradshaw; arguably the first painting including a rail map.
FACING MAIN: 1839 map from the original Bradshaw's: the world's first known national railway network map.

HOW THE RAILWAYS CREATED TIME

Pre–Industrial Revolution, whole towns set their clocks by local sundials, which, subject to the seasons, were often imprecise. During the early 1800s sundials were replaced by an average—or "mean"—time, balanced by a location's longitude (its location east or west from 0 degrees). While almanacs recording mean times sufficed during the stagecoach era (passengers would adjust their watches), rail travel required further precision as people moved over long distances quickly—trains were missed as "local" time was different at the originating station.

In November, 1840, following a series of accidents caused by trains running at "London Time" or "Bristol Time" (a difference of ten minutes), Britain's Great Western Railway introduced a concept called "Railway Time"—effectively making it London Time on the entire network. The system was so successful that it was quickly copied by other British train operators, and later by civic authorities at each locality. Derived from the time set by the Greenwich Royal Observatory, it became known as "Greenwich Mean Time," or GMT. And thanks to telegraph poles erected adjacent to the rail lines, an electronic signal carrying the precise time at Greenwich was sent around the whole country by 1855, making an accurate single time zone applicable to 95 percent of the British Isles.

By 1880 GMT was becoming universally adopted, and just four years later GMT—now known as Coordinated Universal Time (UTC)—became the base reference point for global timekeeping. UTC is still used today. In the US, a series of accidents on long single track (the most serious in 1853 when two New England trains smashed into each other because the guards had different times on their watches, killing fourteen) made standardized time imperative for the survival of the railroads. Although its original champion was a civilian called Charles F. Dowd who in 1870 came up with "A System of National Times for Railroads," it took until 1881 for the General Time Convention (an association of the major rail companies) to agree on its adoption. The GTC secretary William Frederick Allen suggested using approximately fifty local railroad times, with five large time "zones." Though there was opposition, Allen eventually convinced senators of the plan's sense. "Standard Rail Time" began at noon on November 18, 1883, across the United States of America. India switched to "Madras Time" (linked to the Greenwich time signal by telegraph!) in 1906. The rest of the world followed, so time zones are another by-product of railroads.

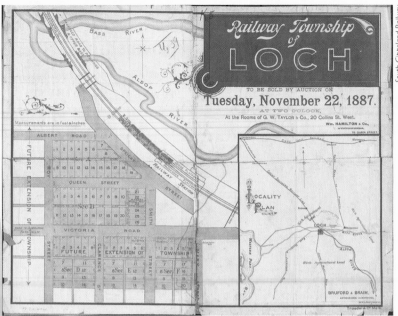

FAR LEFT: 1872 Burlington and Missouri River Railroad Company poster advertising land for sale, across two states.

LEFT: 1887 South Gippsland Railway Company poster promoting the auction of an entire small town-to-be in the Australian state of Victoria. The station did not open for three years.

BELOW: The extent of railways in operation across the Indian Subcontinent by 1908, representing incredible engineering feats in the mountainous northern states.

FACING PAGE: The carving up of land plots around the newly served rail station at Franklin County, Arkansas, 1893. Shaded regions had already been sold prior to the auction.

Rails shaped continents

It's hard to imagine when staring at the expanse of a car-driven city like Los Angeles that the original layout of roads and location of suburbs was entirely due to rail companies (page 47). Dust is the only thing that moves now in Farina, South Australia: once a little town created by the Ghan railroad, virtually nothing is left but the station building itself. Kharagpur in West Bengal was a track junction around which the Bengal-Nagpur Railway Company built a colony to house workers in 1898; today it has a population of 200,000, almost all of whom are working for or connected to the railroad. The station claims the longest railway platform in the world at 1,072.5 meters!

The list of settlements started or heavily influenced by the arrival of the rails would fill a telephone directory–sized book in and of itself, but it's clear that billions of human souls owe their livelihood, their life experiences, and where they physically live, at least in part, to the influence of the railroad. Take work: at their peak in the 1920s, United States rail companies employed over two million people. Even today, over 1,500,000 have a job with Indian Railways—the biggest civil employer in the world.

Railways played a crucial role in the wars of the nineteenth and twentieth centuries: major lines were taken over by the military during the American Civil War, The Trans-Siberian Railway (pages 64–65) transported troops to the Japanese front in 1904 during the Battle of Yalu River, and German railways took concentration camp victims on their final fatal journey during the Second World War. In life and death and all points between, the planet was a rail world for much of its recent existence.

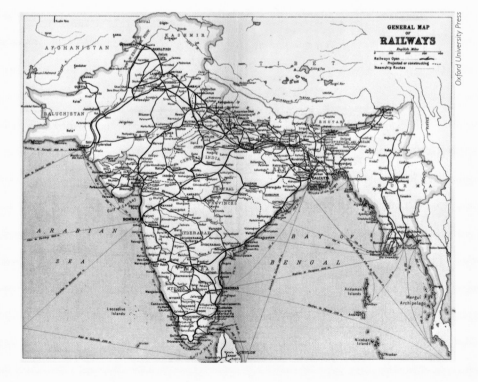

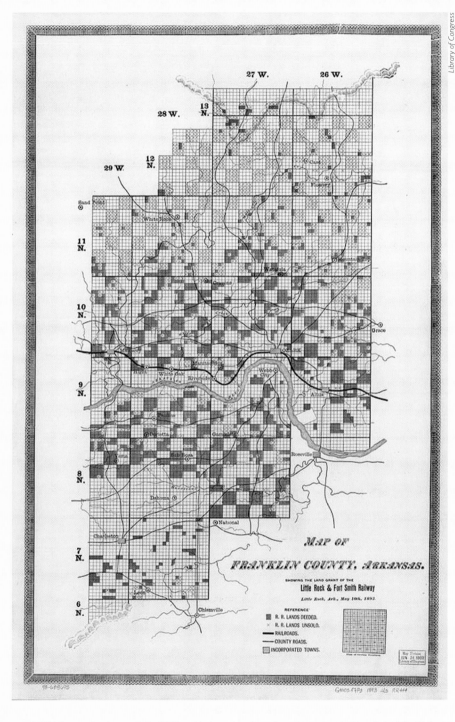

RIGHT: Germany's rail network (in 1910) enabled troops and supplies to be sent to the front during World War I.

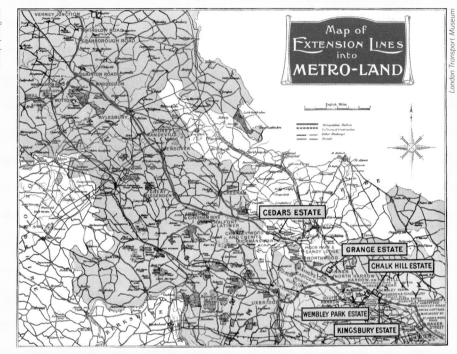

ABOVE: London's "Metro-Land," 1923; entire housing estates were built by the Metropolitan Railway company alongside their stations in open country, in a deliberate attempt to extend the city—and maximize their profits!

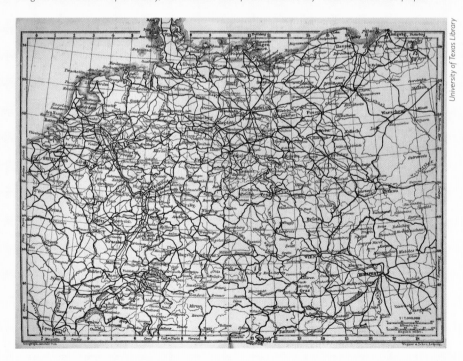

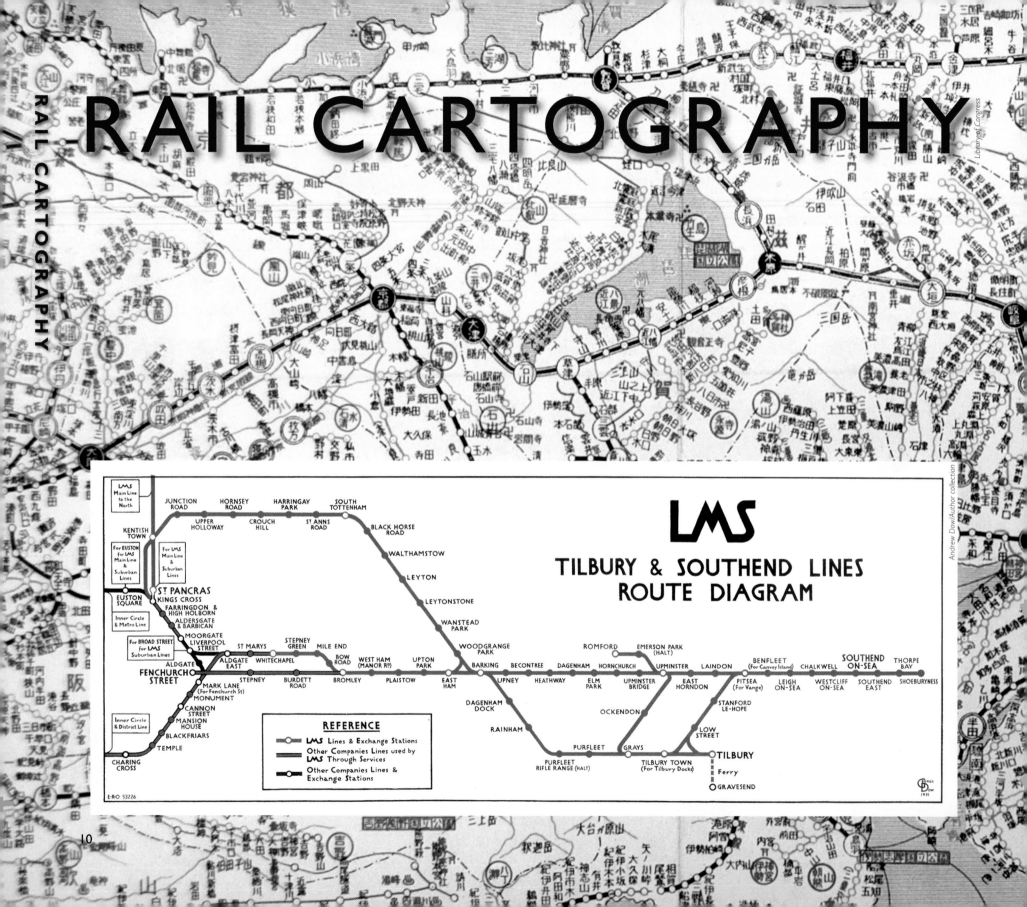

Library of Congress

Andrew Dow/Author collection

LMS

TILBURY & SOUTHEND LINES ROUTE DIAGRAM

LMS Main Line to the North	JUNCTION ROAD	HORNSEY ROAD	HARRINGAY PARK	SOUTH TOTTENHAM					
	UPPER HOLLOWAY	CROUCH HILL	ST ANNS ROAD	BLACK HORSE ROAD					

KENTISH TOWN

For EUSTON for LMS Main Line & Suburban Lines

For LMS Main Line & Suburban Lines

WALTHAMSTOW

ST PANCRAS
KINGS CROSS
FARRINGDON & HIGH HOLBORN

EUSTON SQUARE

LEYTON

Inner Circle & Metro Line

ALDERSGATE & BARBICAN

LEYTONSTONE

MOORGATE
Liverpool Street

For BROAD STREET for LMS Suburban Lines

WANSTEAD PARK

ST MARYS STEPNEY GREEN MILE END

ALDGATE
FENCHURCH STREET

ALDGATE EAST WHITECHAPEL

BOW ROAD

WOODGRANGE PARK

ROMFORD EMERSON PARK (HALT)

SOUTHEND ON-SEA

THORPE BAY

MARK LANE (For Fenchurch St)
MONUMENT

STEPNEY BURDETT ROAD

BROMLEY PLAISTOW

WEST HAM (MANOR Rd) UPTON PARK

BARKING BECONTREE DAGENHAM HORNCHURCH UPMINSTER LAINDON

BENFLEET (For Canvey Island) CHALKWELL

CANNON STREET
MANSION HOUSE

EAST HAM UPNEY HEATHWAY ELM PARK UPMINSTER BRIDGE EAST HORNDON PITSEA (For Vange) LEIGH ON-SEA WESTCLIFF ON-SEA SOUTHEND EAST SHOEBURYNESS

Inner Circle & District Line

BLACKFRIARS

DAGENHAM DOCK

OCKENDON

STANFORD LE-HOPE

TEMPLE

RAINHAM

LOW STREET

CHARING CROSS

PURFLEET GRAYS

TILBURY

PURFLEET RIFLE RANGE (HALT)

TILBURY TOWN (For Tilbury Docks)

Ferry

GRAVESEND

REFERENCE
- ○—○ **LMS** Lines & Exchange Stations
- —— Other Companies Lines used by **LMS** Through Services
- ●—● Other Companies Lines & Exchange Stations

E·R·O 53226

Stingemore
1935

The
POSITION OF
THE RHODESIAS
IN RELATION TO
SOUTHERN AFRICA

Ashworth Collection

SEPTENTRIO

OCCIDENS

ORIENS

MERIDIES

UGANDA

KENYA

MOMBASA

DAR es SALA'AM

BELGIAN
CONGO

ELISABETHVILLE

ZOMBA

LUSAKA

Zambesi River

VICTORIA FALLS

SALISBURY

Zambesi R.

Chobe R.

Okavango R.

BULAWAYO

UMTALI

BEIRA

BEITBRIDGE

BENGUELA

WINDHOEK

Limpopo R.

WALVIS BAY

MAFEKING

PRETORIA

LOURENÇO
MARQUES

JOHANNESBURG

KIMBERLEY

DURBAN

BLOEMFONTEIN

EAST LONDON

CAPE TOWN

PORT ELIZABETH

LEGEND
Railways..........
Roads..............
Airways............

FACING PAGE, LOWER: Mapping the
paths of railroads has taken many
forms, but the simplest way to show
complex and winding routes has been
the schematic. One of the first people
to start looking at rail diagrams was
British cartographer George Dow, now
seen as a pioneer of information design.
His first "Dowagram's" were produced
for the LNER in 1929, this stylish and
clear LMS in-carriage strip map dates
from 1935.

THIS SPREAD: A 1930s guide to
railways produced by the government-
sponsored Japan Travel Bureau. At this
time most Japanese maps were highly
detailed geographic representations of
the land. Japan rapidly developed a
unique style, ranging from some of the
most picturesque panoramic landscapes
to the most brutal simplification of routes
into straight lines between stations.
CENTER: Simplified 1920s map of rail
connections around Rhodesia.

11

N? STANNARD & SON'S, PANORAMIC BIRDS-EYE VIEW OF FRANCE & PRUSSIA
AND THE SURROUNDING COUNTRIES LIKELY TO BE INVOLVED IN THE WAR,
WITH THE RAILWAYS & STRATEGIC POSITIONS OF EACH ARMY, & THE GREAT FORTRESSES OF THE RHINE PROVINCES.

A.M.CASSANDRE

NORD EXPRESS

LONDRES BRUXELLES RIGA
PARIS LIEGE BERLIN VARSOVIE

BELOW: Detail of 1920s railway junction diagram for Portsmouth, England, showing distance in feet, chains, and miles. These were made for the entire country and were especially useful for showing where tracks met.

The point of any map is to somehow shrink a real-life-size three-dimensional, physical space onto a flat piece of paper in two dimensions (or more recently onto a screen) to aid navigation. Though the colorful range of shapes, sizes, and styles seem logical when looking at a finished map, deciding what geographic details to put on or leave off, and where to place text, is crucial to how effective and legible a map will be (not to mention its aesthetic appeal!). Mapping railroads has posed many challenges to cartographers.

After the painstaking and detailed process of surveying the land, engineers make ever more precise sketches of the solutions needed to carry track beds, iron rails, and the weight of locomotives and wagons over the terrain.

Immense engineering challenges are posed by needing to cross valleys, rivers, and mountain ranges; railroads can generally only cope with gentle inclines to negotiate hills. Just think of the complexity and detail needed to get this long thin track bed to be flat and head in the correct direction over sometimes hundreds of kilometers! Accurate terrain sketches are integral to any railway endeavor.

While this was complicated enough in the nineteenth century, consider the difficulty of inserting rail systems into an urban environment, worse still under the city streets. Basements, sewers, wires, and other utilities need to be worked around or moved, meaning precise mapping is absolutely crucial to the entire construction project.

ABOVE & LOWER PANEL DETAIL: Cassandre's classic 1927 poster was not just a beautiful piece of art: it also contained along the bottom a highly stylized cartographic representation of the four major rail routes in to Berlin.
TOP LEFT: 1870 bird's-eye view of Europe by Leventhal.
FACING: 1895, an early attempt by Russian Empire railways to dispense with geographic accuracy of route and replace meanders with straight lines.

LONDRES BRUXELLES RIGA
PARIS LIEGE BERLIN VARSOVIE

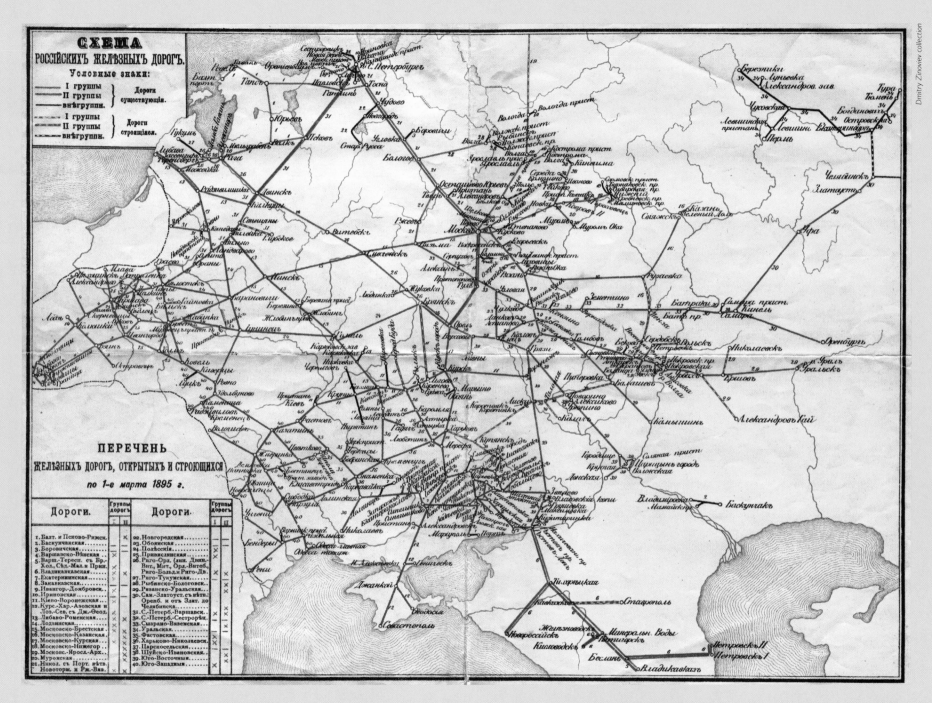

Once a line is built, it isn't just the passengers who might want to know where the trains go; maps have to be produced for the needs of signalers, maintenance staff, landowners, utilities providers, emergency services… this is why such a plethora of mapping styles have evolved for railroads. While the majority of this book focuses on passenger maps, this chapter also includes examples of a range of different approaches to the way railroads are presented, both for internal use (by engineers, etc), as well as those for the public.

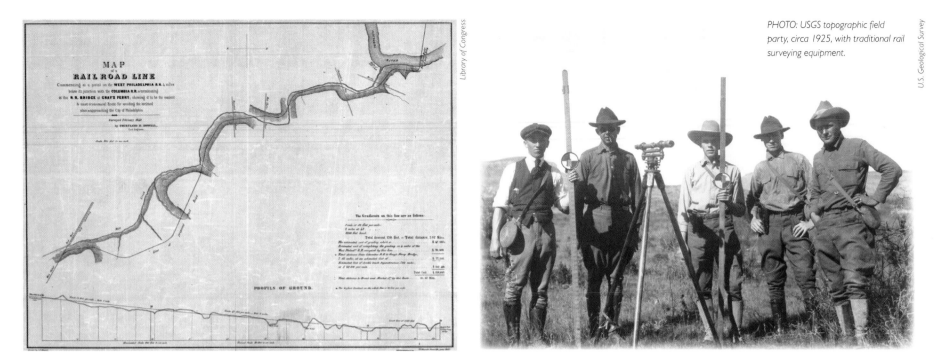

PHOTO: USGS topographic field party, circa 1925, with traditional rail surveying equipment.

ABOVE: The 1849 survey of a 17 km route between Grays Ferry Bridge and connections to the West Philadelphia Railroad.

The pioneering surveyors

FACING TOP: Survey for the 1851 Moscow to Saint Petersburg railroad. BELOW: 1845 survey between New York City and New Haven.

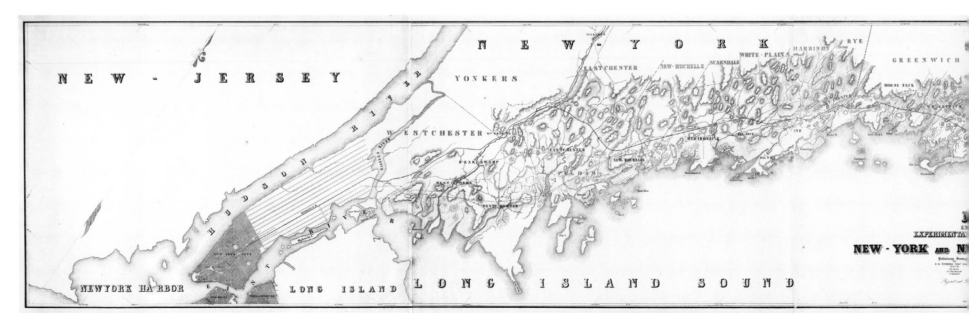

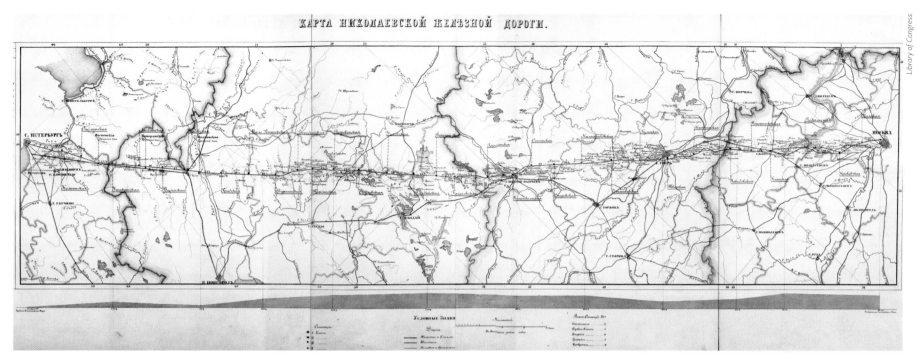

КАРТА НИКОЛАЕВСКОЙ ЖЕЛЂЗНОЙ ДОРОГИ.

Before a single stone is moved, any railroad requires a detailed technical survey of the route. In the early days, it was not uncommon for directors to ask for several routes to be examined: *on foot!* In some parts of the world this meant exploring unknown, even dangerous country.

Disgruntled landowners, canal or toll-road company stooges, anxious locals, Luddites, or even highwaymen were all known to have attacked many a poorly defended railroad surveyor.

Though mapmaking had been improving for centuries, it was the demand to build railroads over uncharted terrain that drove the need for better measuring methods and cartographic accuracy. The triangulation of such vast unmapped spaces as the interior of the Indian Subcontinent, for example, aided both cartographers and rail builders. But it was the great transcontinental railroads (pages 60, 62–63, and 68) that were to bring the greatest advances.

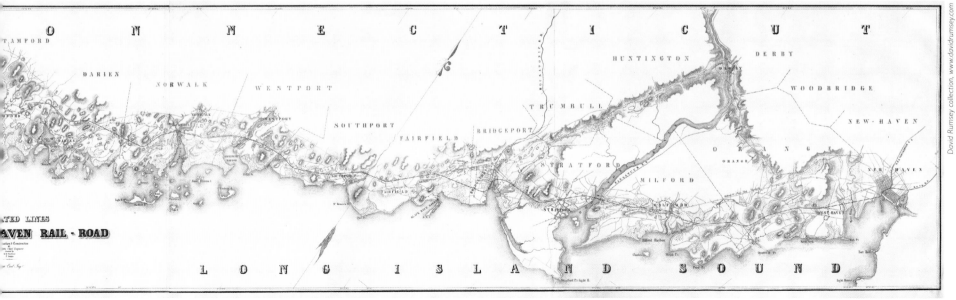

SKELETON MAP

-DINGLE STATION-

MANCHESTER-SHEFFIELD-WATH
ELECTRIFICATION

KEY

MANCHESTER

SHEFFIELD

PROJECTED RAILWAYS

PREPARED IN THE OFFICE OF AMERICAN MILITARY ATTACHE, PEIPING, CHINA. JAN. 15, 1936.

全国铁路
营业站示意图
（货运）

说明

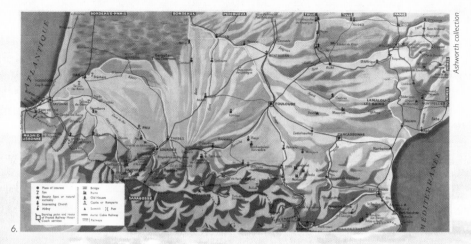

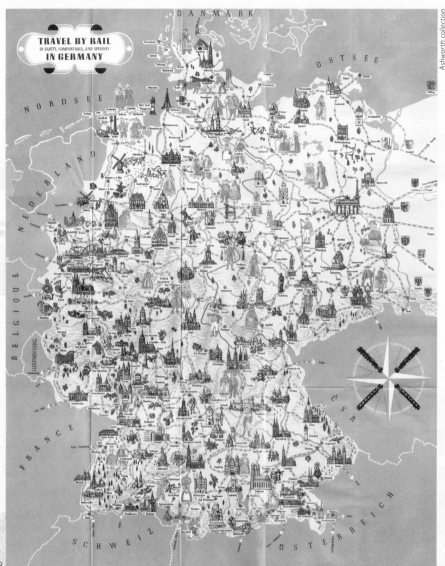

Nº STANNARD & SONS PANORAMIC BIRDS-EYE VIEW OF THE FRENCH & PRUSSIAN PROVINCES,
ON THE BANKS OF THE RHINE.

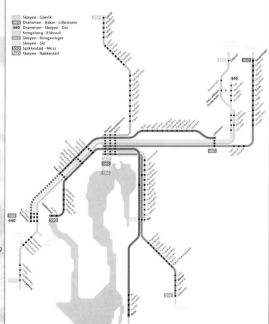

Ashworth collection

Ashworth collection

Norman B. Leventhal Map Center @ Boston Public Library

NSB

Author

12:12 AM 12/12/12

TRAVEL BY RAIL
IN SAFETY, COMFORTABLY, AND SPEEDILY
IN GERMANY

1: 1850 "skeleton" Southern Michigan plan resembles future schematics.

2: 1929 signal box track layout diagram from the Liverpool Overhead Railway.

3: 1954 engineers' diagram of an electrification scheme in northern England.

4: 1936 US military blueprint-style map of projected Chinese railways.

5: Unusual 1982 Chinese schematic removing lines between station dots allows a portrait shape for all China.

6 & BACKGROUNDS: Geographic realism from a 1962 French brochure.

7: "Bird's-eye," "aerial," or "balloon" views (popular 1860–1890) give a perspective impossible until flight and are reminiscent of Google Earth. Usually of just towns, here is all Prussia, in 1870.

8: German routes with exaggerated landmarks, made for 1960s rail tourists.

9: 2010 Oslo suburban services on a classic 45 degree-based schematic, a style used on many urban rail diagrams.

10: Real-time train locators often use Google Earth for background—but not on this Manchester Metrolink mock-up.

Variations on a rail map theme

The examples in this chapter and throughout the book are testimonies to one massive home truth about how railroads are mapped: cartographers' use of every trick available—even inventing some of their own—to convey the supremacy of one route over another, or to clearly demarcate separate routes/stations when many are crowded together, or to make the network fit the available display space. Maps based on geographic features or landmarks are common on tourist guides. More diagrammatic ones are often found inside trains or signal boxes. As the Internet and handheld devices grow in importance, ever more ingenious/3D methods will inevitably be used to guide riders to trains. Many real-time train indicators use existing maps as background but designs are evolving constantly.

Ostentatious Oriental offerings

One of the great joys of collecting rail maps is discovering the diverse and sometimes surprising array of styles chosen to represent routes. Most material is a fair reflection of the culture that surrounds it, so it's no surprise that the Far East has produced some of the widest variations of design.

Art evolved in Japan as early as the tenth millennium BCE, and many of the maps presented here and throughout the book are a testimony to that tradition: intricate, delicate, and outstandingly beautiful.

Developments in the later half of the twentieth century, however—namely the miniaturization of electronics—have led to abstraction and simplification rarely seen in Western maps (and this on the world's most complex rail service patterns and track layouts!).

Yet Kim Ji-hwan's metropolitan area diagrams combining geometry and geography can lead to results that even Beck, Dow, and Vignelli would surely approve of (page 43).

LEFT & BELOW: Panoramic Japan Railways 1928 fold-out map and brochure by Saburo Yoshida using a geographically based bird's-eye view of the Sanyo route around Nagoya and the Kisogawa River. Such attention to detail and beauty is not uncommon on Japanese maps of this period.
FACING, NEAR LEFT: 1897 map of Japanese rail routes with a well-balanced presentation of the different islands that constituted the then Japanese territories.
FACING, FAR RIGHT: 1920s map of all Japanese-influenced railway territory.

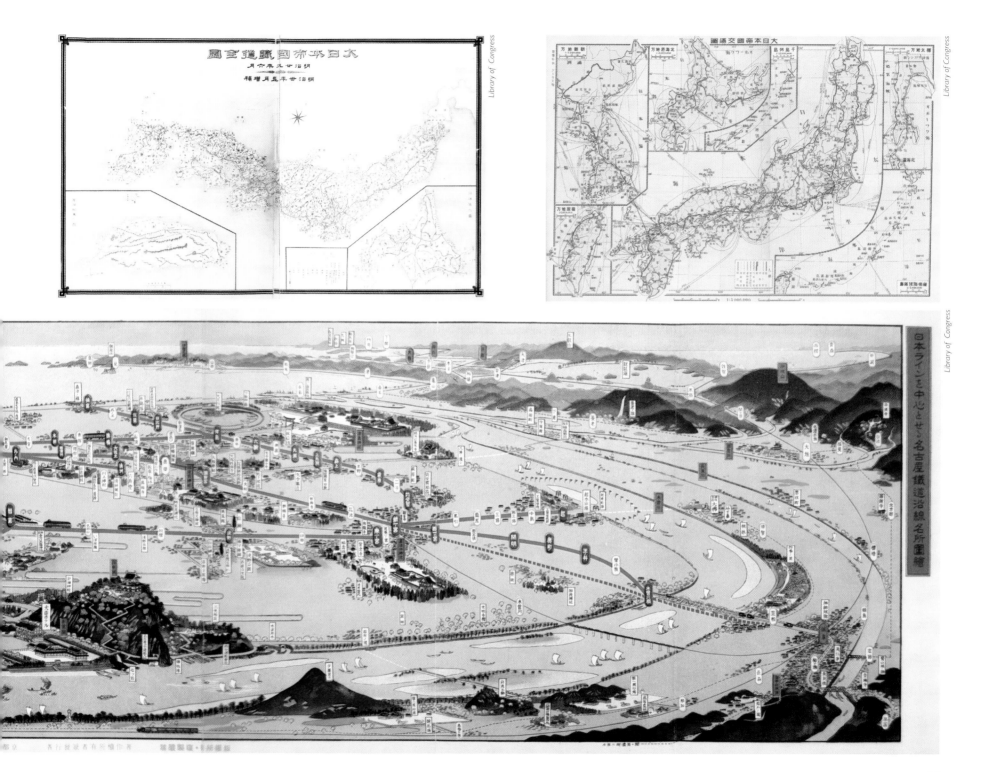

大日本帝國鐵道全圖

大日本帝國交通總圖

日本ラインヲ中心とせ〻名古屋鐵道沿線名所圖繪

20

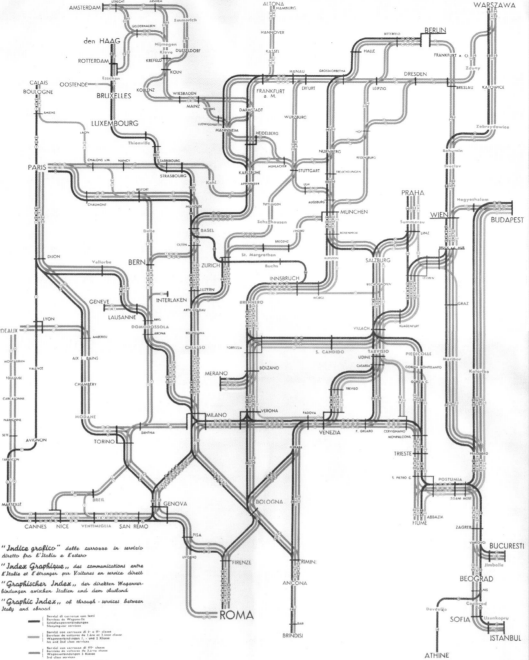

Max Roberts collection

FACING: A perfect example of creative railroad marketing that is both eye-catching while stretching physical accuracy to the nth degree! This is a 1907 British poster designed by Arthur Gunn for the Great Western Railway. The canny graphic juxtaposition of Cornwall to the shape of Italy is both witty and persuasive. Although if the Cornish tree is not sprouting apples, quite how many oranges were to be found growing in damp and chilly Britain is a matter of some artistic license!

CENTER: This beautifully simplistic and stylized Italian view of European connections highlights a common trait of railroad cartography: exaggerating the practicality of a journey. It gives the impression one might hop on a single train anywhere from Istanbul to Amsterdam without a care in the world. In reality during 1938 when this diagram was issued, such a journey would have involved changing trains several times and crossing at least six frontiers. A torturous endurance test for even the biggest train enthusiast!

MERE MARKETING OR PURE PROPAGANDA?

21

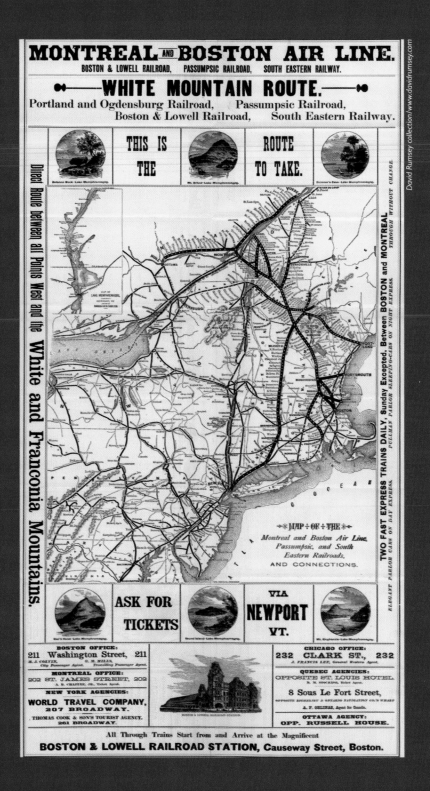

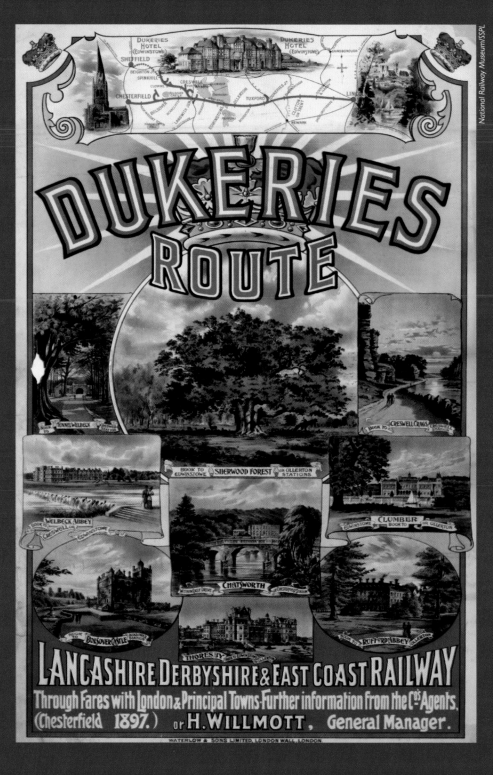

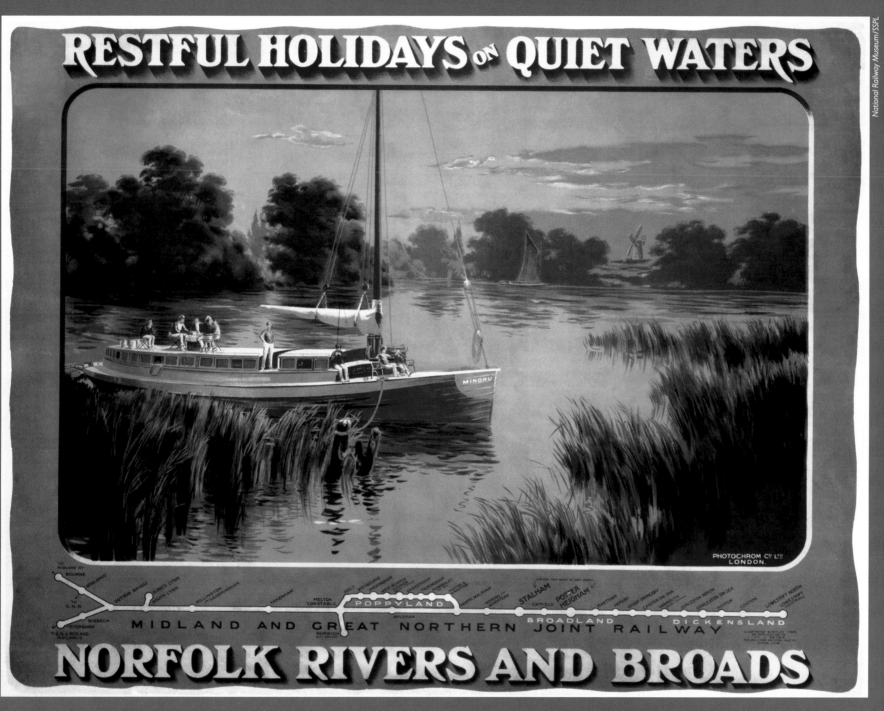

ABOVE Unusual early "strip" diagram on a 1914 British promotional tourist poster for the Norfolk Broads. "Poppyland" and "Dickensland" were both coined by Victorian novelists but the concepts were exploited by railroad marketeers.
FACING LEFT: 1887 Montreal and Boston poster promoting the "White Mountain Route." FACING RIGHT: 1897 Lancashire, Derbyshire and East Coast Railway promoting their idyllic "Dukeries" route between Lincoln and Chesterfield.

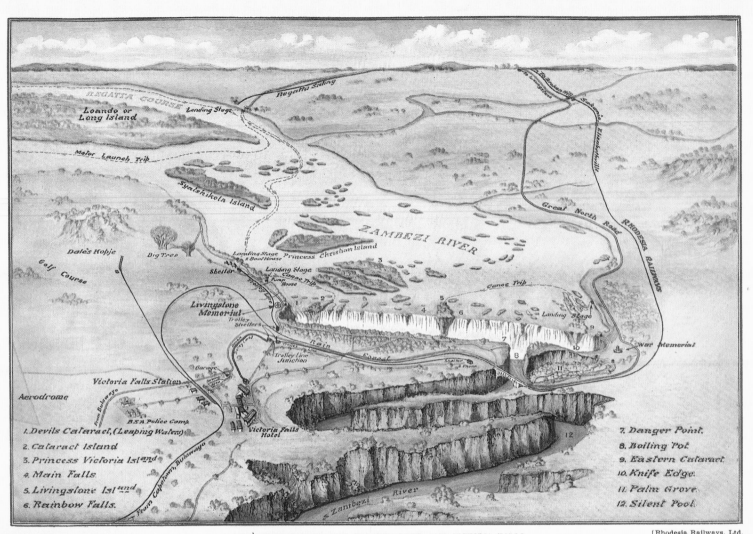

1. Devils Cataract, (Leaping Waters)
2. Cataract Island
3. Princess Victoria Island
4. Main Falls
5. Livingstone Island
6. Rainbow Falls.

7. Danger Point.
8. Boiling Pot
9. Eastern Cataract
10. Knife Edge.
11. Palm Grove.
12. Silent Pool.

A BIRD'S-EYE VIEW OF THE ZAMBEZI RIVER AND VICTORIA FALLS.

[Rhodesia Railways, Ltd.

ABOVE: Thomas Cook letterpress for trains to the 1851 Great Exhibition.

Cartography is nothing if not a series of editorial decisions about how to represent content. What is included or omitted is a compromise between the mapmaker's skill, the constraints of organization, and, occasionally, political agendas. When used to market a rail line—particularly on posters, long appreciated in the travel world as the most effective promotional vehicle—such compromises are amplified.

Incorporating maps on posters blurs the distinction between being simply informative—helping riders locate their destinations—or purely decorative. The most effective are those that combine the two, managing to function as attractive but useful publicity vehicles. Themes range from locations served, sights along the route, quality and speed of service, to touting new trains, bridges, or stations.

The posters featured here are not only exceptional for their intrinsic aesthetic appeal, but because often these efforts improved cartographic skills generally. As was to be expected, the use of posters to market railways was inevitably fiercer where competition between companies was more intense, with each line vying for consumer attention. Hence there were huge numbers of posters produced in Canada, France, the UK, and the USA. That said, state-owned railways, in Belgium, for example, and even those private lines that had secure monopolies in other nations around the world, were keen to embrace the trend of poster-making—if for no other reason than brightening up otherwise dreary station walls.

The use of posters to promote rail travel can be traced back as early as some of the first lines, but the main driver of stylistic improvement was the changes in printing methods during the second half of the nineteenth century.

When railroads began in the 1830s, the most common and cheapest printing technique available was letterpress.

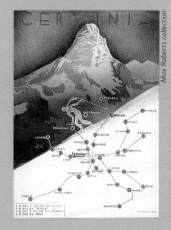

PANORAMA DU MASSIF DU MONT-BLANC ET RÉSEAU DU CHEMIN DE FER AÉRIEN "CHAMONIX-PÈLERINS-AIGUILLE DU MIDI"

FACING TOP: With much artistic license this panoramic representation of Victoria Falls was produced by Rhodesia Railways in the 1920s to encourage tourists deep into Africa.
ABOVE: Mountaineering was one of the leisure activities that drove many thousands to tour the rugged parts of Europe and Canada. This 1930s brochure of European lines into the Alps has a stylized diagram interwoven with the skier.
RIGHT: Early 1920s poster promoting the ease of ascending France's Mont Blanc via the "Réseau du Chemin de Fer Aérien"—a lift offering spectacular views, which opened to riders in 1901.

Mountrains

FACING LOWER RIGHT: An early color lithograph by the PLM for special trains bringing visitors to the opening of the 1889 Exposition Universelle in Paris featuring Gustave Eiffel's "temporary" 300 meter tower!

Thomas Cook & Sons, for example, used letterpress sheets to advertise holidays via the London & North Western Railway "at home and abroad" in 1841! The technique consisted of printing individual posters from rows of (usually wooden) blocks of letters. While images could be scratched onto wooden blocks, the resulting posters were not that pretty. With the popularization of lithography—where ink is applied to etched stone or metal plates—more elaborate graphic designs became possible. Lithography was invented in 1796, but chromolithography (color printing) was not really possible until after 1837; the ease of printing color images would allow railroad poster design to truly blossom.

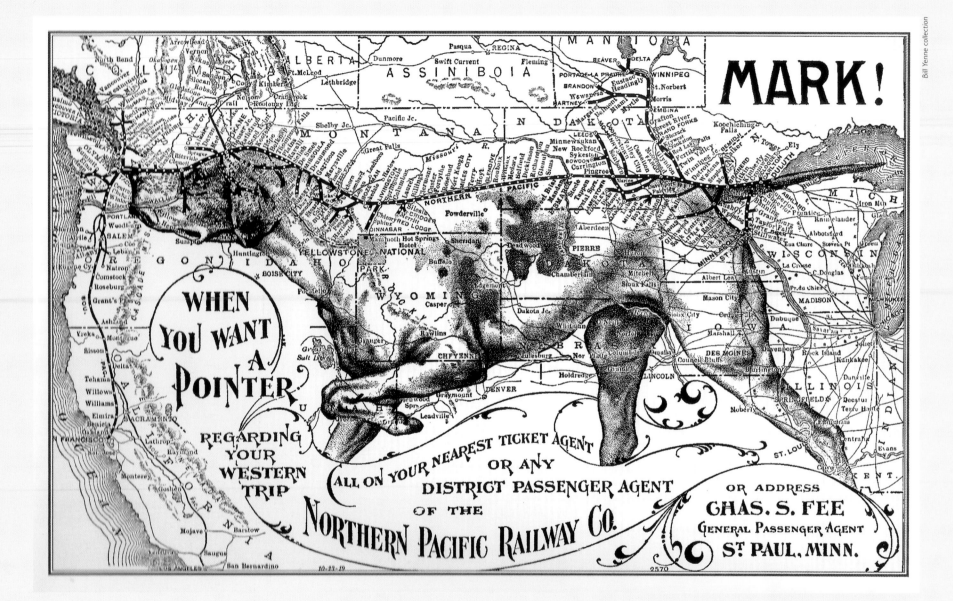

Finally, advances like offset lithography (major inventions came in 1875 and 1903) and photo engraving (from 1863) allowed designers to open their imaginations even further.

The ephemeral nature of the printed poster unexpectedly gave rail cartography its greatest medium for experimentation. Although some early maps were produced on enamel, they had the obvious limitation of being expensive to replace when lines were expanded. Therefore, as improved and inexpensive printing techniques were standardized, cartographers gained the freedom to attempt new styles: schematics, simplification of otherwise complicated geographic meanders, overlays, and downright exaggerations of the landscape—experimentation that would be impossible on geographically accurate maps.

Poster design was quickly raised from a marketing tool to a respected art form, and was exported all over the world: on postcards, travel brochures, timetables, and even tickets, helping in a pre-Internet age to define national/cultural identity. French designers Toulouse-Lautrec and Jules Cheret became highly sought after, and some of the finest early examples of rail posters hail from France. Victorian exhibitions and world fairs—The 1851 Great Exhibition at London's Crystal Palace, the 1889 Paris Exposition Universelle (for which the Eiffel Tower was built), and the 1893 Chicago World's Fair—were all subjects of maps and poster campaigns by rail companies.

Many Victorian and Edwardian maps and posters featured somewhat gargantuan characters looming ominously over landscapes!
FACING: Lighthearted line promotion from inside an 1896 timetable for the NPR. Made by the Poole Brothers studio in Chicago, some distortion of the line trajectory is done in order to accommodate the dog's backbone. Frivolously using animal forms is not historically uncommon in mapmaking.
TOP CENTER: 1907 poster by Alfred Nicholls featuring a game bird often shot in the Scottish Highlands.
BELOW: 1898 fishbone map for a Quebec and Lake Saint John Railway brochure luring fishers onto their trains to the lakes. The stylized fish became an unofficial company logo.
LOWER CENTER: A large clown tempts visitors to the northeast coast of Britain on the cover of a 1911 LNER holidaymakers pamphlet.
FAR RIGHT: 1908 poster with steps representing the "Uganda Railway" (which oddly never even ran through Uganda, but rather British East Africa, which is modern-day Kenya). Perhaps the construction workers were put off by the giant lion?

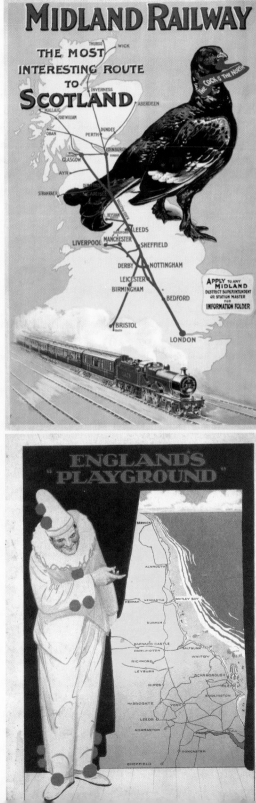

Outsize creature attractions

ABOVE: One of the earliest Canadian Pacific posters, made in 1882, clearly incites settlement on cheap farmland.

Canada calling cowherds

Given the nation's vast size, miles of unspoiled landscapes, and desire to make the most of them, Canadian railway companies produced literally thousands of dynamic posters promoting the country's resources and impressive transit system, many encouraging migration to farm the virgin lands.

The Canadian Pacific (page 63) grew from running a massive railway network to operating luxury resorts, hotels, steamships, and even an airline, churning out over 2,500 posters from the 1880s until 1970, many of which were of exemplary quality and style.

Their evocative images of spacious and enticing lands hung in travel offices and were plastered along station walls throughout cramped and gloomy industrialized countries, and were likely one of the main inspirations for the millions who visited and settled in Canada during the twentieth century.

So many beautiful posters were made in Canada that they have spawned an entire nostalgia industry of ephemera collectors spanning the globe. Maps were featured less frequently on larger posters, but thankfully plenty of pamphlets, brochures, and timetables with maps have survived.

From the end of the nineteenth century until some years after the Second World War, the train had become the most heavily used form of mechanical transport. Over a billion passenger rail journeys were made during 1920 in the USA alone, representing an enormous proportion of the working population with money to spend on travel, not just on going to work but increasingly for leisure purposes.

Luring passersby, in crowded industrialized cities on far-off lands, to travel to the remotest outposts of your country by train—especially convincing them to book a holiday with your company—was a tremendously lucrative business.

The travel boom enhanced the rail poster and vice versa. Companies like the Canadian Pacific Railway proudly trumpeted their ability to carry passengers by train, steamship, *and* plane (page 31)! The leading force behind the entire CPR project, William Van Horne, took charge personally of promoting a new route which opened in 1888, aggressively stating: "If we can't export the scenery we'll import the tourists." The CPR even went so far as to move lock, stock, and barrel—via their services—to take up permanent residence. Full-color posters encouraged people to uproot for the Canadian wilderness.

TOP: 1909 Dutch poster of newly opened electric train lines between Rotterdam and Den Haag.
ABOVE: 1913 Russian postcard montage and map of the Trans-Siberian Chinese Eastern Railway branch.
LOWER CENTER: Michahelle's 1930s poster evoking Goethe's German poem about the land of lemons.
FAR RIGHT: Dating from 1900, when a competing "West Coast" line also existed, this was an example of an early joint effort (by the Great Northern, North Eastern, and North British railways) to promote their "East Coast Route" to Scotland. Portentously, these companies would later amalgamate as the mighty LNER.

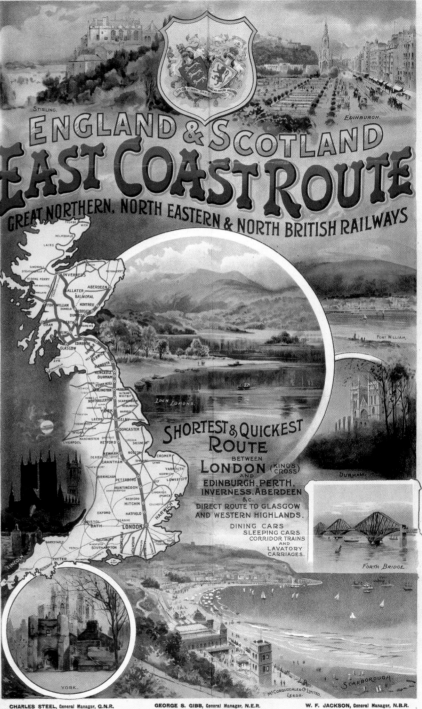

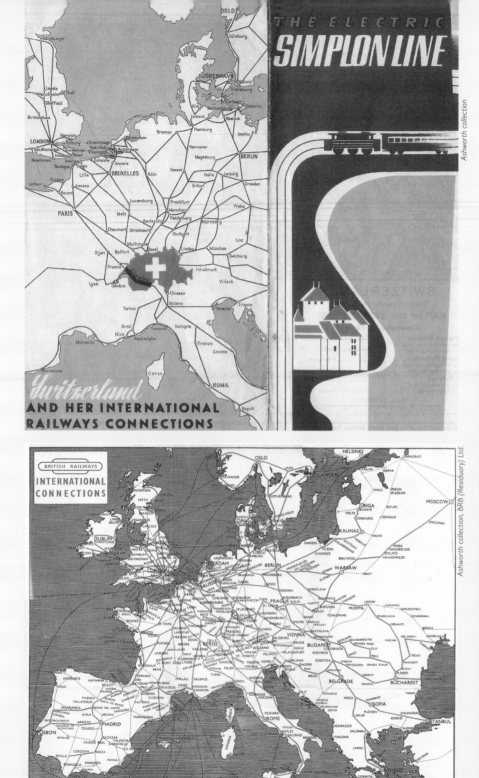

Neighbors' networks

In Western Europe—a crowded continent of many nations with differing track gauges—it's fascinating to see how countries perceived their position in relation to others, and how they chose to promote that to potential visitors. From Italy's stylish diagrams (page 21) to the colorful view from the Caucasus, most maps stressed the apparent simplicity of international passenger travel—though this was rarely so easy when changing trains or getting ferries at frontiers.

LEFT: 1950s Swiss heart of Europe.
BELOW: 1930s Czech view of Europe.
LOWER LEFT: European connections from Britain in 1953.
LOWER RIGHT: How Spain's RENFE showed its European links in 1958.
FACING NEAR: 1931 Canadian Pacific rail, sea, and air routes to Europe.
FACING LOWER RIGHT: 1937 map and timetable of London-Italy services.

"British Boys: learn how to own your farm in Canada" and claims about the practicality of a local railroad was the CPR's constant tease on posters. Another was: "Special farms on virgin soil near the railway" (page 34). It worked! Immigration to Canada boomed in the nineteenth century.

The need to revamp print design emerged in the 1930s with the introduction of new rail technology: sleek modern-looking streamlined locos like the Burlington *Zephyr* (1934), the *Hiawatha* of America's Milwaukee Road (from 1935), the British *Mallard* (world steam record speed of 203 km/h in 1938), and the deluxe *South Wind Keystone* of the Pennsylvania all helped to refocus attention back to railroads. These technological advancements provided new promotional and marketing inspiration, and the early twentieth century was to become the heyday of the travel print designer.

The work of a good rail publicity artist was elevated to a professional level. Sascha Maurer, already a distinguished originator of beautifully evocative rail posters, wrote during the 1930s that it was "the greatest ambition of every commercial artist to design travel posters."

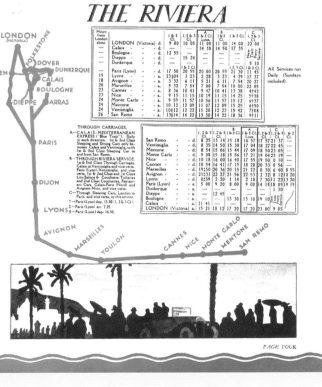

North American peaks

Several rail construction boom periods occurred across North America: some of the first poster-sized maps showing railroads snaking across the entire USA during the mid- to late 1800s inspired both pioneers and passengers. The zenith was 1916, when the US achieved over 408,000 km (and 1.7 million employees), but the golden age was the decade following 1940. Although the Depression resulted in line closures, the Second World War reinvigorated rail. Old steam locos were replaced by modern streamlined diesels, the economy was booming, and operating revenues in 1943–45 were more than double those of 1930. This led to an explosion in mapping and advertising services: thousands of local guides were produced and rail operators in both Canada and the USA invested heavily in publicity abroad.

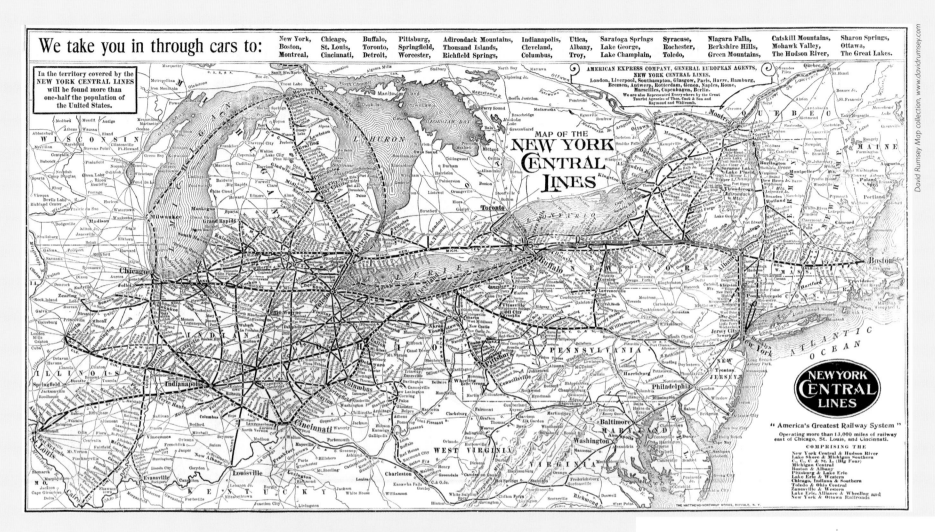

We take you in through cars to:

| New York, Boston, Montreal, | Chicago, St. Louis, Cincinnati, | Buffalo, Toronto, Detroit, | Pittsburg, Springfield, Worcester, | Adirondack Mountains, Thousand Islands, Richfield Springs, | Indianapolis, Cleveland, Columbus, | Utica, Albany, Troy, | Saratoga Springs, Lake George, Lake Champlain, | Syracuse, Rochester, Toledo, | Niagara Falls, Berkshire Hills, Green Mountains, | Catskill Mountains, Mohawk Valley, The Hudson River, | Sharon Springs, Ottawa, The Great Lakes. |

In the territory covered by the NEW YORK CENTRAL LINES will be found more than one-half the population of the United States.

MAP OF THE
NEW YORK
CENTRAL
LINES

AMERICAN EXPRESS COMPANY, GENERAL EUROPEAN AGENTS, NEW YORK CENTRAL LINES.
London, Liverpool, Southampton, Glasgow, Paris, Havre, Hamburg, Bremen, Antwerp, Rotterdam, Genoa, Naples, Rome, Marseilles, Copenhagen, Berlin.
We are also Represented Everywhere by the Great Tourist Agencies of Thos. Cook & Son and Raymond and Whitcomb.

NEW YORK
CENTRAL
LINES

"America's Greatest Railway System"
Operating more than 13,000 miles of railway east of Chicago, St. Louis, and Cincinnati.

COMPRISING THE
New York Central & Hudson River
Lake Shore & Michigan Southern
C., C. C. & St. L. (Big Four)
Michigan Central
Boston & Albany
Pittsburg & Lake Erie
Lake Erie & Western
Chicago, Indiana & Southern
Toledo & Ohio Central
Zanesville & Western
Lake Erie, Alliance & Wheeling and
New York & Ottawa Railroads.

THE MATTHEWS-NORTHRUP WORKS, BUFFALO, N.Y.

ABOVE: 1918 eastern USA map by the New York Central lines when track was at its absolute maximum.
RIGHT: Detail from an 1882 New York Central poster—early encouragement for using railways to get to the coast.
FACING: 1883 wall poster map from the Chicago and Alton Railroad: even by this relatively early date, much of the US population was served by rail.

New York Central & Hudson River and Boston & Albany Railroads.
MAP OF THE
SEA SHORE AND SUMMER RESORTS of NEW YORK AND NEW ENGLAND.

Celebrated designers in Europe included Frenchman Henri Biais and Ukrainian Adolphe Mouron Cassandre, working for Chemin de Fer du Nord; Hugo D'Alesi and Robert Falcucci (Paris-Lyon-Méditerranée); German-born Ludwig Hohlwein; Scandinavian Freda Lingstrom; and Dutchman Anton Van Anroody. There were also the prolific Brits: Frank Newbould, Tom Purvis, and Norman Wilkinson. North America bequeathed the revered Edward McKnight Kauffer, Leslie Ragan, Maurice Logan (of the Southern Pacific), Hernando G. Villa (Sante Fe), and Canada's esteemed Peter Ewart and Norman Fraser. Australia gave us James Northfield. These and other railroad commercial artists at one time included some form of map on their images and were also some of the earliest adopters of in-house graphics: many logos, typeface standardizations, and stylized maps stem from this period.

ABOVE: A completely fabricated 1920s artistic impression of a Canadian landscape, deliberately propagated to encourage tourists.
BELOW: This 1920 poster by David Allen was made for the Canadian Pacific Railway, which was trying to entice new settlers to relocate.
LOWER CENTER: In the great race across Canada the Canadian Pacific was winning the publicity battle. Here all routes appear to run via them —although of course other service providers like the Canadian National also had cross-country lines.
TOP RIGHT: A 1923 Southern Pacific poster is not shy about its reputation.

The need for easily identifiable graphic "devices" arose from the stiff competition between private companies, like America's Rock Island logo, the North Western's red bull's-eye (both seen from 1901), and the Sante Fe cross and logotype (early 1910s), Britain's GWR lettering (1905), the French PLM logo (from 1902) etc. But the integration of maps into railroad marketing was to go hand in hand with this early "corporate identity" from then onwards, though sometimes—particularly as new networks arrived in developing countries—good design has not always kept up with the need for providing speedy service information.

Many maps achieved an iconic status of their own, the most famous example being the London Underground diagram, which was so revered that permission was rarely granted for its use outside its primary job as a map. Printing one clever abstraction of the design onto a three-sheet poster by Lilian Dring was halted entirely in 1933. Such protectionism was most certainly not the case with main line and suburban railroad maps. Though there were less "classic" maps to copy, ruin, or overexpose by their inclusion on posters, arty use of main line map elements was seen as a much better driver of new and repeat traffic than was the case with local rapid transit system maps, and was often positively encouraged.

Given the intrinsic nature of cartography to require decisions about what information to include and what to leave off, rail maps have become the perfect vehicles for propaganda. Beyond the requirements of mere marketing (relatively benign elimination of competing networks), some cartographic editing has had far more sinister implications: advocating the supremacy of one lifestyle over another, or lying about the position of frontiers between opposing states.

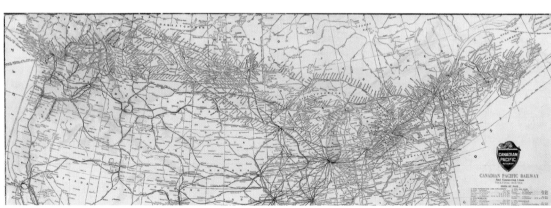

Chemins de fer du Nord

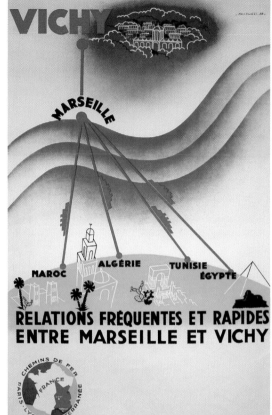

Robert Falcucci

FCDE Cataluna

Many operators saw the benefit of advertising services and attractions outside their own territory.
TOP: A 1920s joint Belgian, French, and British poster using a simplified map of services for routes from the French-speaking lands to "au coeur de l'Angleterre" (the heart of Britain).
TOP CENTER: Stylish 1932 poster by celebrated Corsican designer Robert Falcucci. The PLM rail company was keen to entice visits to the Maghreb and Egypt, which were under heavy French influence during this period.
RIGHT: 1950s poster encouraging Spanish interior city dwellers to leave the pollution behind for the fresh air of Catalonia's beaches.

In times of war or periods of heightened political tension, railroad maps have played their part in the partisan aspirations or propaganda of opposing sides.

Thanks to the mapping of colonial South America, Africa, and the Middle East for long rail projects (realized and not), "unclaimed" lands became territories, all because of a map. The early 1900s plan for a Berlin-to-Baghdad railway was frequently touted as proof of German industrial might.

Another poignant example of cartography's role in propaganda was the frenetic drive during the cold war for satellite mapping of the interiors of Russia and China and publicizing, sometimes erroneously, their expansionist intentions. Here the location of man-made rail tracks, highly visible from space, led to vast amounts of cartographic data being produced by the American military for strategic purposes. Yet more trickery was the complete erasure of West Berlin from some East Berlin urban rail maps (page 39). Thankfully such cartographic fibs are becoming rarer.

NORTH EASTERN RAILWAY

The TEES PORTS, HARTLEPOOL and MIDDLESBROUGH & The RAILWAY CONNECTIONS.

Particulars of Dock Charges, Railway Rates and General Facilities can be obtained from:
HARTLEPOOL: THE DISTRICT GOODS AND DOCK MANAGER, NORTH EASTERN RAILWAY, WEST HARTLEPOOL.
MIDDLESBROUGH: THE DISTRICT GOODS MANAGER, NORTH EASTERN RAILWAY, DARLINGTON.

EXPLORE LINCOLNSHIRE BY L·N·E·R
IT'S QUICKER BY RAIL
Illustrated Booklets and Full Information from L·N·E·R Offices and Agencies

Great Western Railway

SUNNY SOUTH WALES
THE COUNTRY OF CASTLES
GENIAL CLIMATE

SEND FOR ILLUSTRATED BOOKLET (Post Free) FROM SECRETARY SOUTH WALES COAST RESORTS ASSOCIATION PORTHCAWL GLAMORGAN

FELIX J.C. POLE, General Manager.

Eye in the sky

With such a rich rail heritage, the British Isles have, over 200 years, been squeezed, distorted, and twisted cartographically into a myriad of shapes and sizes, creating some of the world's most iconic rail maps and posters. Bird's-eye views have existed since mapping first evolved but its popularity grew in the 1500s (city views of Venice, 1550, and Frankfurt, 1552), with the Turgot map of Paris (1730) and again in the 1850s (Effingham Wilson's *A Balloon view of London as seen from Hampstead*, 1851). The style was adopted by many British rail cartographers and utilized worldwide as it had the advantage of allowing a large area to be compressed into an aesthetically pleasing and practical, if geographically implausible, space.

FAR LEFT: 1909 bird's-eye view of Teeside.
TOP: Montague Black's 1934 bird's-eye view of Lincolnshire, one of a series of six LNER panoramic landscapes.
CENTER: Idyllic Welsh views and aerial map of the valleys from an early 1920s GWR poster.

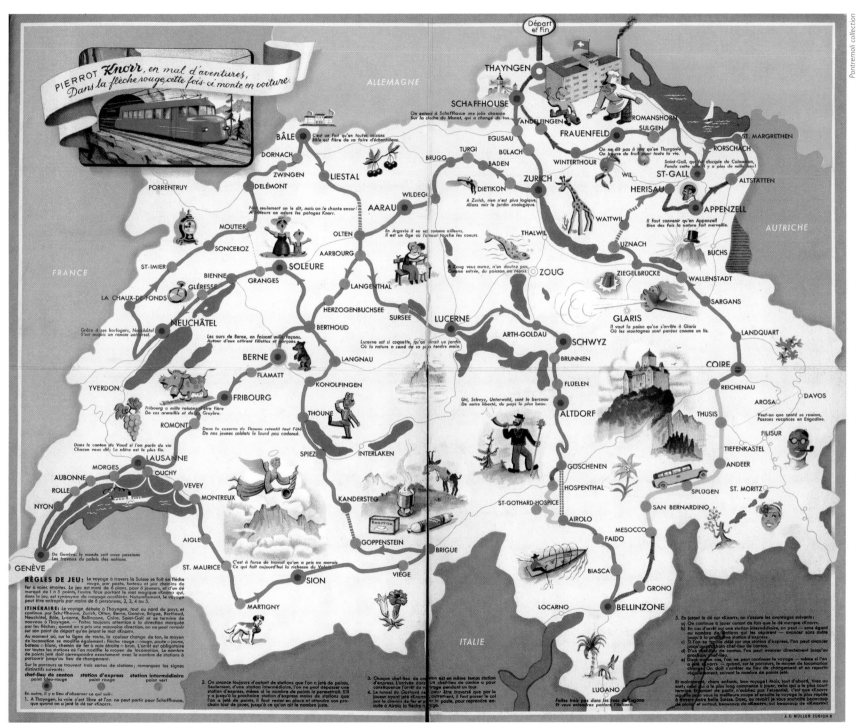

ABOVE: Simplified Swiss lines turned into a 1940s child's board game. This outstanding ephemera was produced by food manufacturers Knorr, but what kid big or small could resist giraffes and angels over the snow-clad Alps?

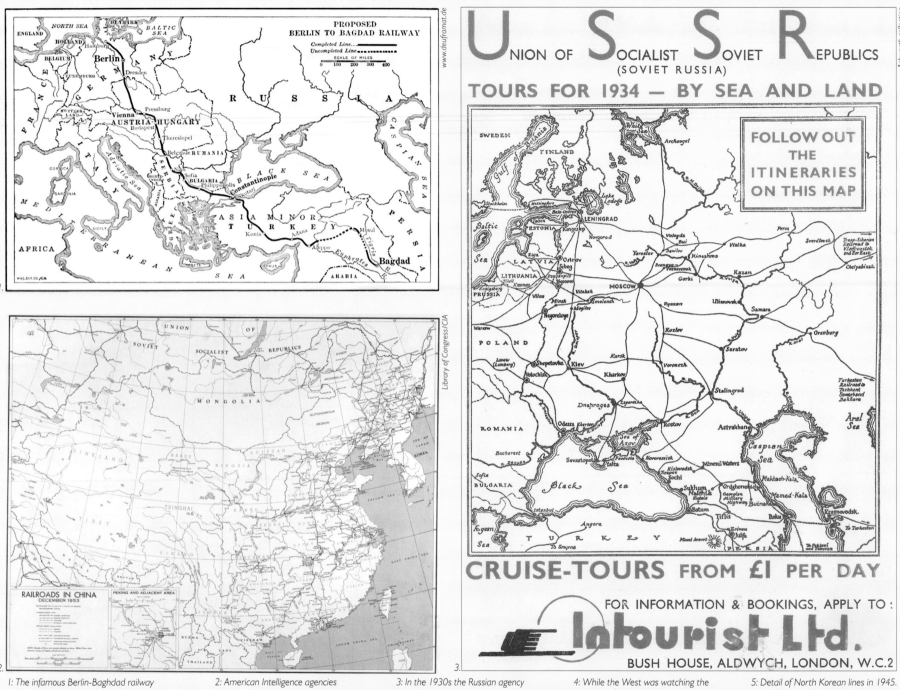

PROPOSED
BERLIN TO BAGDAD RAILWAY

Completed Line
Uncompleted Line

SCALE OF MILES
0   100   200   300   400

U S S R

UNION OF SOCIALIST SOVIET REPUBLICS
(SOVIET RUSSIA)

TOURS FOR 1934 — BY SEA AND LAND

FOLLOW OUT
THE
ITINERARIES
ON THIS MAP

CRUISE-TOURS FROM £1 PER DAY

FOR INFORMATION & BOOKINGS, APPLY TO:

Intourist Ltd.

BUSH HOUSE, ALDWYCH, LONDON, W.C.2

RAILROADS IN CHINA
DECEMBER 1953

PEKING AND ADJACENT AREA

1: The infamous Berlin-Baghdad railway cited by some as one of the causes of the First World War due to the German advantage in resource supply.

2: American Intelligence agencies thoroughly mapped many countries during the cold war, as this 1953 study of Chinese railroads proves.

3: In the 1930s the Russian agency Intourist actively sought sympathetic Brits to sample Soviet-style rail travel—though only on "approved" routes.

4: While the West was watching the East, Russian intelligence was making its own maps of the world. Here a 1959 Russian map of Canadian railroads.

5: Detail of North Korean lines in 1945.

6: 1955 American map of "aggressive" Soviet railroad construction in China.

7: 1988 East Berlin's "edited" rail lines.

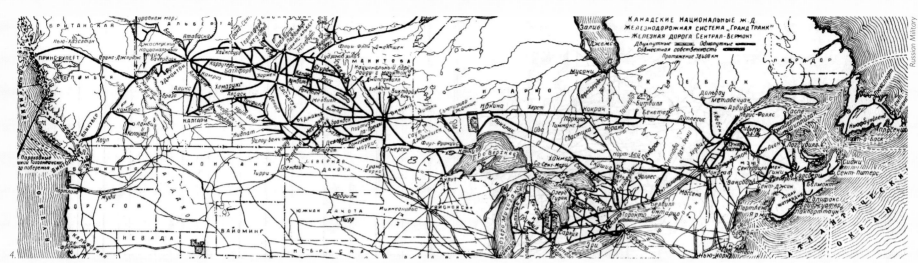

4.

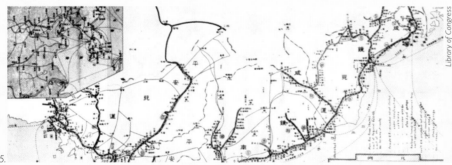

5.

CartograFibs 1: Political agenda's

Misrepresentation of the world around us is nothing new in mapmaking: it's virtually inherent in the art, and as American academic Mark Monmonier puts it, "the arrogant partitioning of Africa in the eighteenth century...putting feuding tribes in the same colony [arbitrarily drawing lines on a map] was a recipe for insurrection and genocide." Concealing a neighboring territory, plotting an enemy's railroads, or using maps to win wars; all have been de rigeur in the politically charged subtext of certain rail cartography. But the 1988 diagram of suburban and U-Bahn services around East Berlin takes the prize for sheer barefaced nerve: by crafty design, the whole of West Berlin and all its train services are squished up so that it virtually disappears, and even the trains around the left edge (only accessible with a Nebenkarte ticket) appear, at first glance, seamlessly stitched into a continuous East Berlin network.

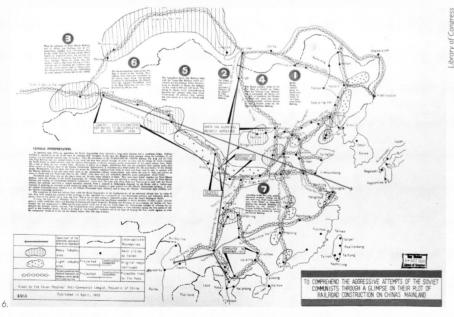

6.

7.

CartograFibs 2: Edits

All maps are selective, but competing railroad companies have long embraced the power of a map to "emphasize" their lines over others that may be available. This is done by artistically leaving out competitors' routes or stations, or in some cases barefaced cartographic fibs are employed to exaggerate the benefits of one service or route over another. Editing information on a map can sway a consumers' perspective—and their money.

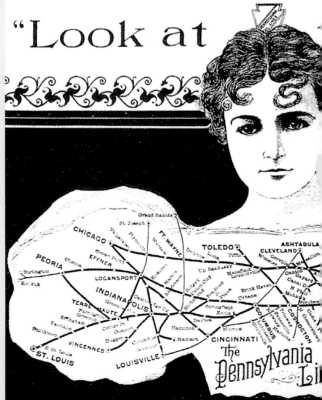

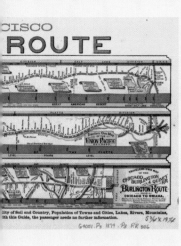

BELOW: Ludicrous shoulder
pads from 1876 Pennsylvania.
ABOVE: 1879 hybrid diagram
and relief map across America.
RIGHT: 1889 Franco-Russian
diagram simplifying routes.
FACING: 1911 selective semi-
relief view of the LNWR lines.

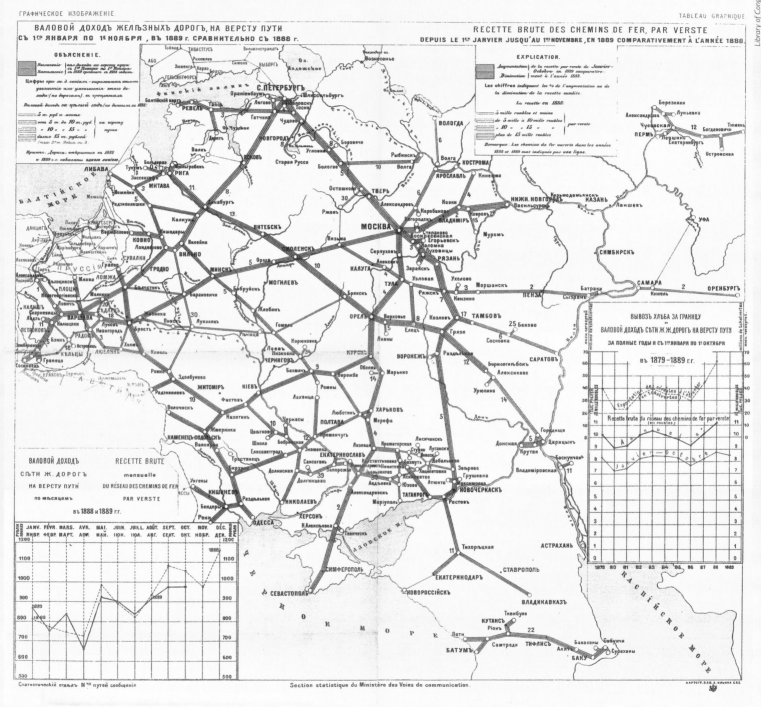

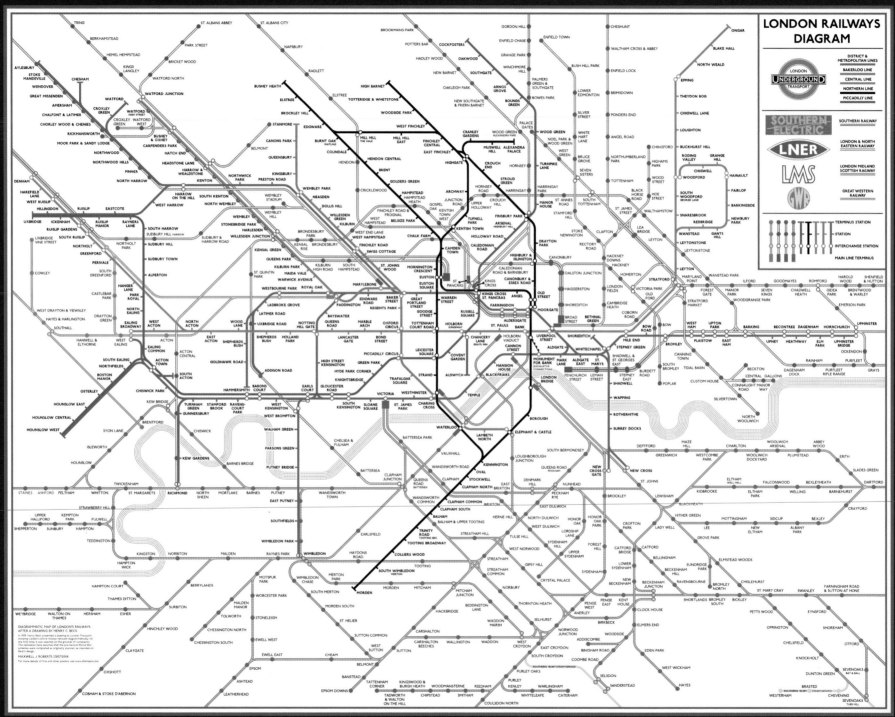

ABOVE: *Legendary London Tube map designer Harry Beck massively distorted the city to squeeze in all railways operating (and planned) in 1938. Never before published, this was digitally remastered/colored by Max Roberts in 2008.*

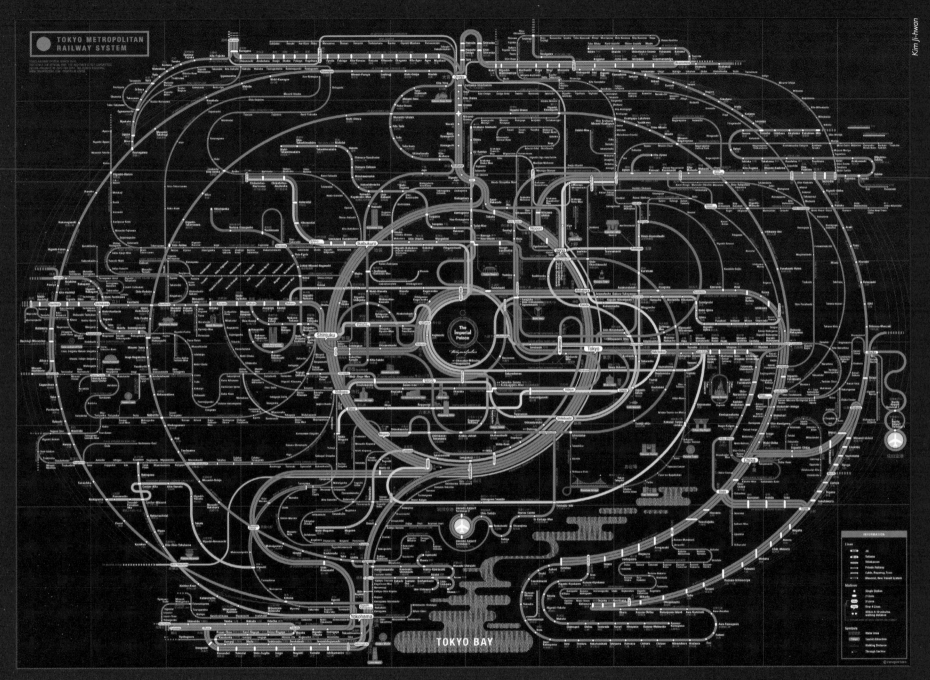

Cartogra*Fibs* 3: Geometry

One of the world's greatest rail maps was Harry Beck's 1933 London Tube diagram. His heavy-rail contemporary was George Dow (page 10). Drawing straight lines between stations—as opposed to true curves—is a trick with cartographic roots dating back to the very earliest lines (page 2). But Beck and Dow should not be understated: their geometric concepts were emulated worldwide, and with computer-aided design and highly creative minds, the art is evolving some stunning new ideas, like Kim Ji-hwan's outstanding 2009 Tokyo region rail map (above). An homage to curvaceousness!

43

CENTER: Abandoned rail bridge in Polish Silesia. Such massive structures were easier to leave standing, becoming monuments to past glories.
THIS SPREAD: Modern high-speed train set manufactured by Bombardier, who have made huge inroads into supplying new rolling stock around the world, especially fast-growing China.

Jan Slavik

Bombardier

WESTERN DECLINE AND EASTERN PROMISE

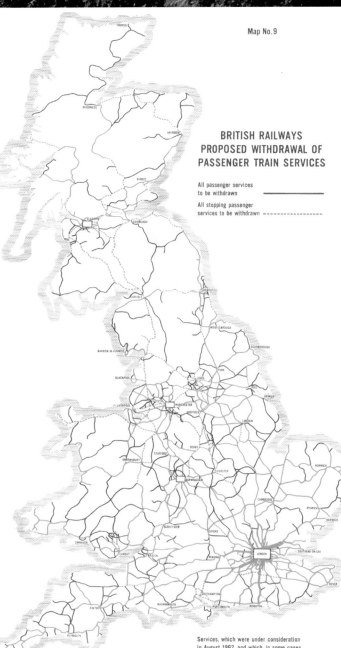

Map No.9

BRB (Residuary) Ltd.

**BRITISH RAILWAYS
PROPOSED WITHDRAWAL OF
PASSENGER TRAIN SERVICES**

All passenger services
to be withdrawn ——————————

All stopping passenger
services to be withdrawn ---------------

Services, which were under consideration
in August 1962, and which, in some cases,
have already been withdrawn, are included
in this map.

CENTER: Dr Richard Beeching cut
the 1963 UK network of 30,350 km
(6,000 stations) to just 19,312 km
(serving 2,128 stations) in less than
a decade; two-thirds of all the routes
and just one-third of the stations were
left! Many other countries suffered
similar fates, as shown in this chapter,
but as the baton of manufacturing and
economic power passes eastwards,
Japan, China, India, and South Korea
are now embarked upon massive
programs of new railroad construction.

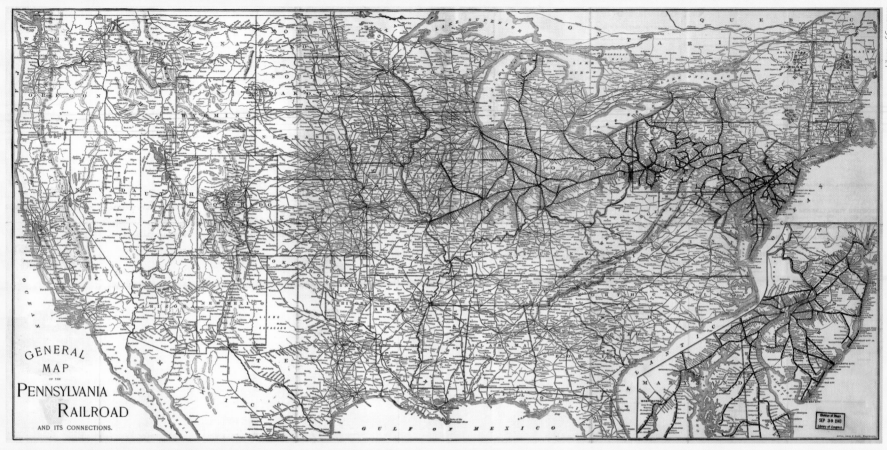

Library of Congress

Wiped off the map

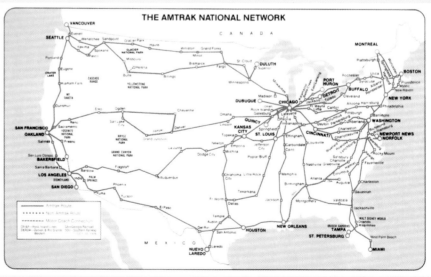

Amtrak

THE AMTRAK NATIONAL NETWORK

The world's biggest railroad network (408,833 km of track and more than 40,000 stations) had been built by competing companies with private money, but by the 1930s the US federal government was paying for the construction of the National Highway System. Rail riders and freight were lured to other forms of transit. Railroads were heavily taxed, dogged by restrictions, and had their speeds limited by the Interstate Commerce Commission (ICC). A long-desired merger of the New York Central and the Pennsylvania could have changed fortunes in the potentially profitable Northeast but by the time the Penn Central was finally created in 1968 (with the New York, Newhaven and Hartford thrown in by the ICC) it was in such a decrepit state and so burdened with outmoded practices that it quickly became bankrupt in June 1970—the largest corporate crash to that date.

The ripples shot round the US, causing many others to halt passenger services, cutting hundreds of cities off the rail map overnight. The government was forced to create Amtrak (nationalization, effectively), which meekly offered a reduced passenger service linking 400 cities from 1971.

Though many freight tracks survived, some heritage and private lines remained open, and some cities and states operated suburban services. The fact that Amtrak still barely serves 500 stations across 34,000 km of tracks is a sad reflection of the world's once mightiest railroad system; a testament to the power of the automotive industry and the triumph of lost opportunities over common sense.

FACING, TOP: 1893 map from a key player in the Northeast, the PR, showing just how dense rail penetration had become even by then.
FACING, LOWER: The first route map of the nationalized Amtrak passenger services from a 1971 brochure.
TOP: 1906 detail of streetcar tracks (red, yellow, and green) shows the density of routes in downtown Los Angeles at that time.
TOP RIGHT: 1912 map of all rails (except LAR) in Los Angeles County.
ABOVE: Amtrak's first logo from 1971.

Since railroads arrived at different periods of economic development, they were already in decline in some countries while booms were being experienced in others.

The first mass rail closure was conceived as early as 1925. By that point, in addition to the 408,000-plus km of heavy rail track in the US, most cities across North America were traversed by streetcar and trolley tracks (over 72,400 km). Private automobile manufacturers quite rightly saw the effectiveness and popularity of these as a natural brake on their own expansion. In what became a national scandal, hundreds of streetcar operations were purchased and deliberately run down during the 1930s, 1940s, and 1950s: millions were forced to buy an automobile. Massive interurban "freeways" were constructed—many right over old rail tracks—and the auto was undeniably in the ascendency.

The situation for "tramways" (as streetcars are called in Europe), was not dissimilar. The first major British system to be dismantled was in Manchester (420 km, closed by 1949), closely followed by London, Leeds, and 200 other towns.

Streetcar desire terminated

The abandonment of electric railroads in Los Angeles was not untypical, but the closure of the streetcar network here seems more acute because it was a city built and laid out *specifically* for public transit. At their height, the Pacific Electric Railway operated "Red Cars," the Los Angeles Railway "Yellow Cars," and the olive green cars of the Los Angeles Pacific ran local, suburban, and interurban services throughout Los Angeles County on over 1,600 km of track. The rail companies even subsidized their own services by acting as realtors, buying land alongside tracks and reselling it to individuals. Naturally thousands of lives depended upon the network to get to and from work and to see their friends and families; people would hop on and off different company streetcars for a seamless journey. Rails were at the heart of urban California and the majority of other US cities.

During the 1930s most systems were progressively bought up, gradually run down, and finally closed by Pacific City Line—part of National City Line (which took over almost 100 streetcar systems across 45 North American cities and replaced them with General Motors buses between 1936 and 1950). NCL was accused of being in the pay of the oil, tire, and automobile industry, resulting in a conspiracy theory and court case called the "General Motors Streetcar Scandal."

As streetcar and trolley lines were replaced by buses, and freeways were constructed across LA, people stranded in far-flung suburbs were effectively forced to buy their own private vehicles during the 1950s and 1960s—a period known as *autotopia*. The last LA streetcar ran in 1963.

Canada chills

Canada's government financially supported rail services earlier than its southern neighbors. Much development had occurred by the 1920s (page 63) but the far western ends of the Intercolonial and Grand Trunk were experiencing difficulties, partly due to the expense of building routes through mainly uninhabited areas, so they were amalgamated to form the publicly owned Canadian National company, which provided a viable competitor to the still privately owned Canadian Pacific. Freight was always a major proportion of income, but due to the rise of the auto and ease of air travel, passenger numbers plummeted from the 1950s onwards: between the 1970s and 1990s thousands of kilometers of track and stations were abandoned, notably in Saskatchewan, Newfoundland, and Nova Scotia. Passenger services have been operated by ViaRail since 1976, yet 40 percent of those were cut in 1981 and a further 55 percent sliced off in 1990. Yet more services were dropped just four years later.

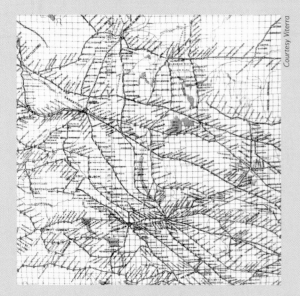

TOP LEFT: Much of the old Intercolonial was abandoned sixty years after this 1907 map when hundreds of stations were closed.

LOWER LEFT: Though this book mainly covers passenger transit, freight played an important role in rail development and mapping. The massive skein of lines penetrating the Canadian prairies was built to link the grain silos to the outside world. However, 60 percent were cut between 1962 and 1998 (the "Western Canadian Branchline Abandonment"), causing big transportation cost increases for farmers, and many more lines and services have gone since then.

ABOVE PAIR: Though a handful of the rail lines shown in the Intercontinental (upper left) and Elevator systems (lower right) maps are still open for freight, the two details (above) from David Marlor's excellent schematic of all Canada's passenger services (in full on page 87) show how few places a train can be boarded in the two comparative areas in 2011. They highlight, in effect, a complete decimation of passenger rail services in much of Canada.

The last major one, Glasgow, shut in 1962, leaving just seaside Blackpool with trams. Only three of the original ninety-odd town tramways survived in France (Lille, Marseille, St.-Etienne), just three were left in Sweden, and one in India. They were removed completely from places like Spain (the last from Zaragoza in 1976), over 100 were shut in Brazil, all sixty were closed in Chile, Australia's fifteen were cut, nine in Algeria, all were closed in the Philippines, South Korea, and Thailand—leaving cities engraved with thousands of kilometers of unused steel rail tracks running down their streets.

The demise was echoed on heavy railways, which had suffered chronic underinvestment since their inception and/ or were exhausted by overuse during the Second World War. Although a handful of isolated modernizations were carried out in some countries—particularly on express and long-distance routes—and despite their use by millions of passengers, it was dark days indeed for the railroads in the 1950s, 1960s, and 1970s. Argentina almost lost its entire network. Rails were mercilessly abandoned across Africa. Another badly affected was Britain. The "Beeching Axe" fell in 1962–63 and by the end of the decade almost a third shut. New Zealand also lost a third of its tracks (2,200 km cut from an original 5,700). France closed more than half of its 60,000 km (and almost lost much more in 1995). The Belgian Chemins de Fer Vicinaux, the world's most dense interurban network, was completely decimated. It went from around 4,811 km in 1945 to less than 250 km by 1970, and a mere 68 km connecting the coastal towns remains in operation today.

Alongside the decline of the urban streetcar in America, the main lines were being strangled there by bureaucracy and bad management. Despite the introduction of streamlined lightweight trains on many routes from the 1930s onwards, other forms of transport, notably the airplane, started to take their toll on long-distance journey passenger revenues.

A frantic period of takeovers and consolidations was started after the ICC approved the Norfolk & Western merger with the Virginian Railway in 1959. Three large companies were joined in 1961 to form the Great Northern Pacific and Burlington: with almost 40,000 km, it became the second largest network in the USA.

Such amalgamations did little to halt the hemorrhaging of passenger numbers till a point when the only thing keeping some trains running was legal obligations from previous agreements. Freight was sustaining operations but also losing to road transit, so when the railroad post offices were stopped in the 1960s the rail companies were crippled. Eventually the American state was forced to set up a structure to take control of the passenger rail services (Amtrak), a situation not uncommon elsewhere. The picture, however, was not entirely bleak: small pointers to change were in the air as older systems tried to modernize, and the key to this was around a huge leap in improving speed.

Ashworth collection

Ashworth collection

BRB (Residuary) Ltd.

BRITISH RAILWAYS BOARD

The Reshaping of British Railways

PART 2: MAPS

LONDON

HER MAJESTY'S STATIONERY OFFICE

Paul Holroyd collection

BRITISH RAILWAYS

WITHDRAWAL OF PASSENGER TRAINS

Halifax—Bradford—Keighley via Queensbury

As from the 23rd May, 1955, the passenger train service will be withdrawn from the Halifax—Bradford—Keighley, via Queensbury branches. The stations concerned are:—

CLAYTON	HALIFAX	WILSDEN
CULLINGWORTH	(North Bridge)	OVENDEN
DENHOLME	HOLMFIELD	QUEENSBURY
GREAT HORTON	INGROW	THORNTON
	(East)	

Queensbury, Denholme, Wilsden and Clayton stations will be converted to unstaffed public delivery sidings for freight traffic, and Ovenden station will be closed entirely.

NOTE.—The passenger train services Halifax—Bradford, via Low Moor and Bradford—Keighley, via Shipley, will continue as at present.

Britain *Beeched*

The backbone of Britain during not one but two world wars, the railroad infrastructure by 1945 was clapped-out, dirty, and in desperate need of modernization. Despite 1948's nationalization, a brave attempt to slap a lick of paint up and some attractive new signage (page V), major investment in track and rolling stock was needed. Some improvements did occur (e.g. the West Coast line electrification, begun in 1959— then soon halted), but the country was virtually bankrupted by war and more drastic action was necessary.

Perversely, private income was growing; by the late 1950s road improvements and car ownership were eating into rail patronage, and running steam trains was a labor-intensive operation. Something had to give. Dr. Richard Beeching, the British Railways chairman, initiated a weeklong traffic study (ending April 23, 1962) which showed that 30 percent of the track was carrying just 1 percent of passengers and freight; half of all stations contributed just 2 percent of income. While he proposed some improvements, Beeching's legacy was closing a massive 9,700 km of branch (and a few main) lines.

LEFT: The 1949 UK route map just one year after nationalization when the network was largely intact but tired.
ABOVE: A foretaste of what was to come: the 1955 closure of one British Railway's branch in Yorkshire. Almost 2000 km had already been closed before the Beeching axe fell in 1963.
TOP: Cover of the maps section of the infamous 1963 Beeching Report—the main map from inside this report showing proposed closures is shown on page 45.
TOP CENTER: The British Rail network by 1981–82: under Mrs. Thatcher's anti-rail government, this was the network at its lowest ebb. The UK was only narrowly saved from the Serpell proposals to cut back on even more.

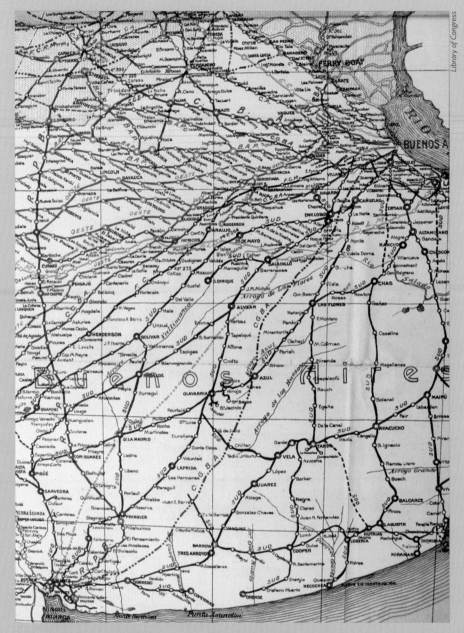

Red de Ferrocarriles Argentinos
Año 1989

Red de Ferrocarriles Argentinos
Año 2001

Crying for Argentina

As a former colony, Argentina had a relatively early start with railroads (1857) and benefited from one of the largest systems in Latin America: over 47,000 km of route by 1920. Following years of widespread closures, privatizations, and cutbacks like the 1990 scrapping of intercity services, the network reached its lowest level in 2001. It now claims 34,059 km, but not all is in active service.

LEFT: Detail of the mass of railroads emanating from Buenos Aires in 1914.
INNER LEFT: The entire country as late as 1989; though in poor condition, most lines were still operational.
INNER RIGHT: Following closures and privatizations, this was the sorry state of passenger rail services in Argentina by 2001.
PHOTO TOP: Abandoned route north of the old station of Elisia. Note the use of three rails either side: this was to accommodate trains that had come from different track gauges.

Another motor for rail bouncing back on the world stage has been the massive growth in the previously underdeveloped countries (particularly China). More recently, greater awareness of environmental issues has been a major influence on resurrecting the fortunes of rail.

Though some progress was made improving the speed of steam locos in the 1930s (test trains like the German *Borsig DRG* beat the 200 kph barrier in 1936 and the infamous British *Mallard* touched 202.6 kph in 1938), scheduled services never really equaled the test runs (the fastest being the British *Cheltenham Express*, top speed of 128.8 kph from 1932, and the US *Morning Hiawatha*, going at 161 kph in 1939).

A handful of experimental ideas were also tried, like the French hovercraft engine trains (1966–67), rocket-propelled locos, and the New York Central's *RDC-3* (1966), which had jet airplane engines strapped onto the roof! All attained speeds of over 300 kph (one at Chevilly, France, even racing to 430 kph). Needless to say, none saw passenger service!

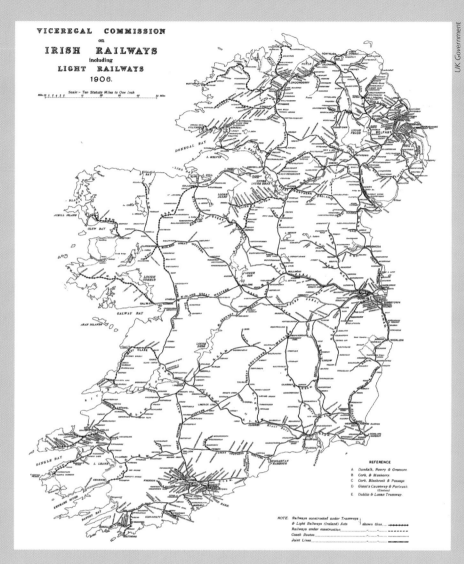

UK Government

VICEREGAL COMMISSION
on
IRISH RAILWAYS
including
LIGHT RAILWAYS
1906.

Scale:— Ten Statute Miles to One Inch

REFERENCE

A   Dundalk, Newry & Greenore.
B   Cork, & Muskerry.
C   Cork, Blackrock & Passage.
D   Giant's Causeway & Portrush.
E   Dublin & Lucan Tramway.

NOTE. Railways constructed under Tramways
& Light Railways (Ireland) Acts   shown thus
Railways under construction
Coach Routes
Joint Lines

Iarnród Éireann

Ireland

————— C.I.E. Passenger Train Services
〰〰〰 Passenger Train Services operated jointly by C.I.E. and N.I.R.
〰〰〰 Passenger Train Services operated by N.I.R.

ABOVE: High fares and fees caused an official inquiry into Irish rail operation, hence the Viceregal produced this now famous map of services in July 1906.

When Irish eyes stop smiling

There were once 5,600 km of track on the relatively small island of Eire, giving it at that time a density of service almost on a par with Germany, Belgium, Switzerland, or Britain. Although 3,237 km remain (intercity lines and commuter routes around Dublin and Cork), most branch lines and rural services were closed between 1950 and 1975. The concentration of lines to and from Dublin earned the network the nickname of "PaleRail."

ABOVE: By 1970 the extent of cuts is clear. All routes radiated from Dublin except the cross-country Waterford–Sligo which limped on, but later closed.

But it was the electric multiple units and diesel-electrics that were to prove their practicality carrying riders at speed. Though some experimentation took place in Germany as early as 1903 (an AEG engine reaching 210 kph that year), it was the Japanese and the French who invested heavily in new train technology during the 1960s and each reaped economic rewards for their country.

On March 30, 1963, a *Class 1000 Shinkansen* whisked along a brand-new track, specially built for high-speed trains, in Odawara, Japan, at 256 kph. The age of the passenger "bullet train" (as it was dubbed because of the shape of its nose) had truly begun.

Japanese bullet fires to the future

In the late 1950s and early 1960s, while Western countries were falling over themselves to scale back their rail networks, the farsighted head of Japanese Railways had a very different vision. The idea of *dangan ressha* (trains as fast as a bullet) had been knocking about since the 1930s, but it was shelved during the war. After six years of construction on a new line between Tokyo and Osaka, the 210 kph *Tōkaidō Shinkansen* train began service in October 1964, just in time for the Olympic Games.

The streamlined engine was the greatest leap forward in rail transit since the steam engines of the 1830s. Following its immediate success (carrying its 100 millionth passenger by 1967), the government passed the Construction of Nationwide High Speed Railways law and started building routes capable of faster speeds from November 1971.

Today with over 2,460 km of lines, virtually every major Japanese population center is now connected to 300 kph services. The effectiveness of high-speed rail in boosting train patronage, cutting pollution, and invigorating the economy is widely acknowledged and is being emulated worldwide.

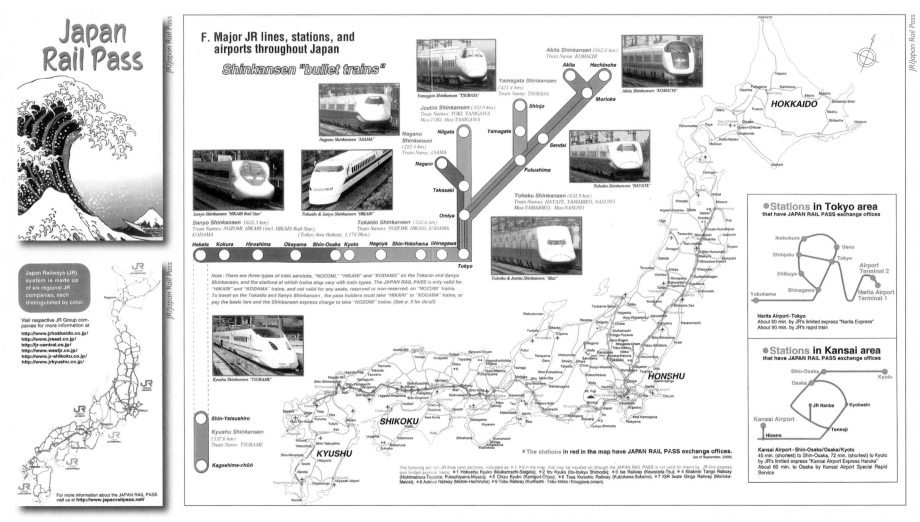

The *Shinkansens* in regular service got faster and faster (319 kph by 1979), but the French were on their tail. 380 kph was reached on the SNCF's southeast TGV service in 1981. Average regular runs between Paris and Lyon slashed a previous five-hour, 512 km journey to 1:55 on a specially constructed 409 km track, decimating air travel between the two largest cities! France subsequently embarked upon a vast civil engineering program that culminated in the Channel Tunnel under the sea to the UK (1994) and now boasts 1,700 km of high-speed lines (with another 2,000 km in construction and planned by the year 2020).

Daily services from Paris take just three hours to get to the Mediterranean (Marseille, 770 km), and newer trains have kept France in pole position. The Germans and Spanish soon followed the French. An experimental German *InterCityExpress* (ICE) reached 406 kph in 1988, and a network of 1,300 km high-speed lines is rapidly connecting the formerly split nation. Spain's high-speed *AVE* now runs on 1,272 km of track with a network radiating out of Madrid and operator RENFE plans up to 6,000 km of fast track by 2020.

China's economic boom has enabled it to whiz ahead of even Europe. First, a 1990s "speed-up" enabled conventional trains to run faster on 6,000 km of track. Then an entirely new 922 km between Wuhan and Guangzhou began operating at 312 kph. But China is spending *$300 billion* by 2020 on a network that will see high-speed trains connecting every large population center with a staggering 25,000 km of track! Italy (814 km), Taiwan (335), Turkey (245), South Korea (240), Belgium (214), the UK (109), and the Netherlands (100) all have high-speed trains now, and a long list (at last including the US) have active plans for thousands more kilometers of high-speed routes (see Trackstats, page 134).

Despite the global evolution, France keeps ahead of the game: on a new section of track between Paris and Metz, the absolute land speed record for a train was broken in 2007 when a TGV zoomed to 574.8 kph—almost a kilometer in six seconds. Though their new AGV (*Automotrice à Grande Vitesse*) trains will average a "mere" 360 kph in service, it will still be possible to traverse the country in less than three hours!

Such speeds put mid-distance high-speed train journeys on a competitive par with air travel (because of the amount of time taken to get to out-of-town airports and all the palaver of security and checking in, etc.). Recent investment is highlighting the otherwise relatively dilapidated state of many of the world's existing conventional-speed railways; but this is incentivizing a myriad replacement/upgrades/improvements.

Reliability, safety, practicality, and environmentally sound credentials are causing a twenty-first-century rail renaissance.

CENTER: The Indian Subcontinent had been crossed by rail since 1871. LOWER RIGHT: 2010 unofficial diagram of the entire Indian Railways system by Arun Ganesh. BELOW: Cover of 1920s state tourist guide with Taj Mahal illustration.

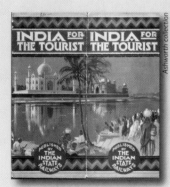

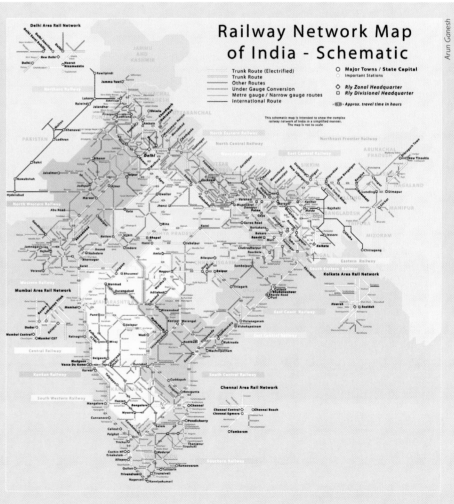

India's new dawn

The majority of India's railroads were built under colonial rule from 1853, but given their importance to the country and the pride it has for rail, some growth has occurred since and a high-speed network is under consideration. After Independence in 1947 there were forty-two companies operating on 55,000 km of track and while some branches were inevitably closed since nationalization in 1951, Indian Railways, the world's largest employer (1.6 million), is still growing and now runs on 63,140 km of track, carrying seven billion passenger journeys a year.

A Red star is born

国家高速公路网布局方案

CRH/China Ministry of Railways

国家高速公路网布局方案

放射线
1. 北京－上海
2. 北京－台北
3. 北京－港澳
4. 北京－昆明
5. 北京－拉萨
6. 北京－乌鲁木齐
7. 北京－哈尔滨

纵线
1. 鹤岗－大连
2. 沈阳－海口
3. 长春－深圳
4. 济南－广州
5. 大庆－广州
6. 二连浩特－广州
7. 包头－茂名
8. 兰州－海口
9. 重庆－昆明

横线
1. 绥芬河－满洲里
2. 珲春－乌兰浩特
3. 丹东－锡林浩特
4. 荣成－乌海
5. 青岛－银川
6. 青岛－兰州
7. 连云港－霍尔果斯
8. 南京－洛阳
9. 上海－西安
10. 上海－成都
11. 上海－重庆
12. 杭州－瑞丽
13. 上海－昆明
14. 福州－银川
15. 泉州－南宁
16. 厦门－成都
17. 汕头－昆明
18. 广州－昆明

图 例
- 首都放射线
- 纵线
- 横线
- 联络线（纵）
- 联络线（横）
- 地区环线

FACING PAGE: China's tracks in 1960. Black lines were built, red dashed lines are the planned routes.
ABOVE: How China's rail system should look by 2012.
FAR RIGHT: One of China's new high-speed trains built for CRH by Bombardier.

The rail network in China stretched for 35,000 km by the mid-1970s, and there were impressive plans (in red on facing-page map) for expansion, especially toward the more remote western side of the country.

Few would have predicted then, though, that China would later begin such a frenetic period of unprecedented economic growth and would more than double its track (86,000 km by 2009) to become one of the world leaders in high-speed rail.

China is now set for over 3,676 km of high-speed rail to be in operation by the end of 2010 and has firm plans to build an unprecedented 25,000 km *more* ready for 2020! Given the tenacity and preparedness of the Chinese government and its people for monumental achievements, it seems entirely possible that CRH will achieve its ambitious target, giving China the largest high-speed rail network in the world.

Bombardier

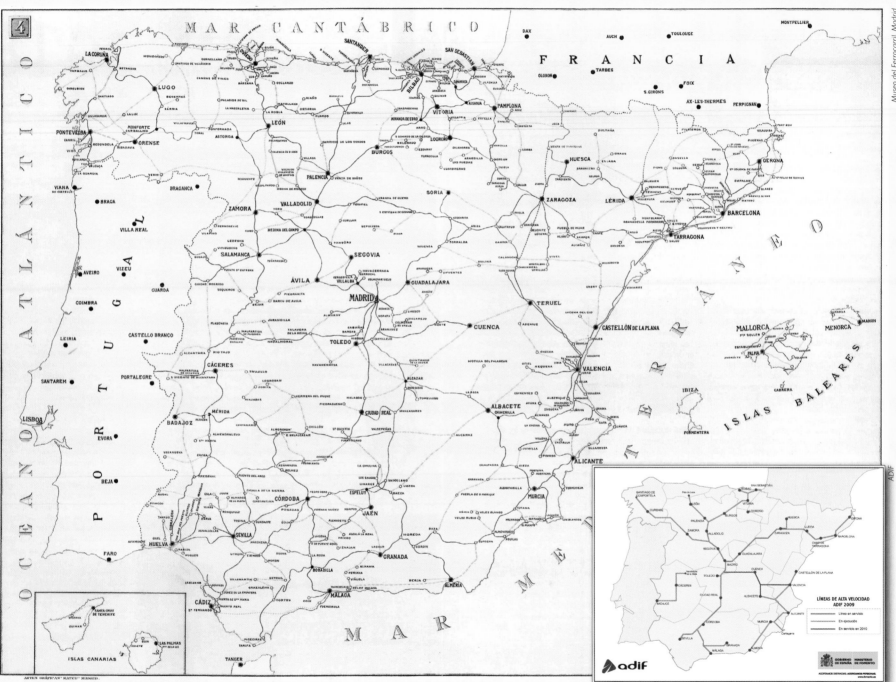

A.V.E. Maria

Since laying the first tracks between Barcelona and nearby Mataró in 1848, Spain embraced railways, but they were run down by the 1970s. It was not until 1992 that the first high-speed line, called AVE (between Madrid and Seville), caused such a revival that Spain now wants Europe's biggest high-speed train network.

ABOVE MAIN: All rails in Spain, 1918. INSET: 2010 Spanish high-speed AVE routes and their connections.

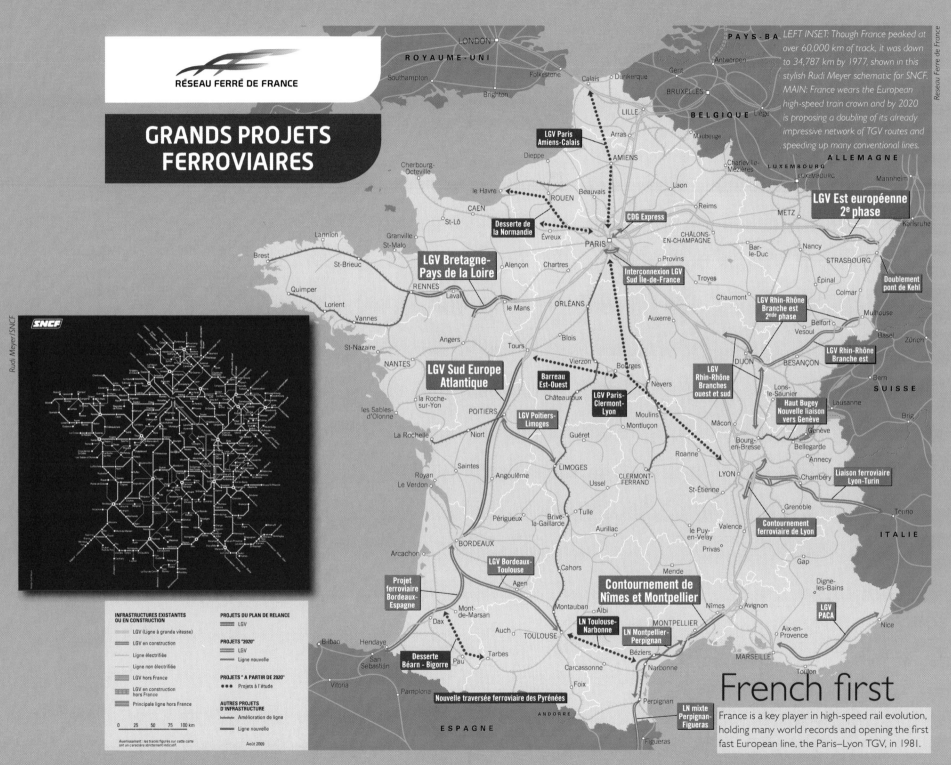

LEFT INSET: Though France peaked at over 60,000 km of track, it was down to 34,787 km by 1977, shown in this stylish Rudi Meyer schematic for SNCF. MAIN: France wears the European high-speed train crown and by 2020 is proposing a doubling of its already impressive network of TGV routes and speeding up many conventional lines.

French first

France is a key player in high-speed rail evolution, holding many world records and opening the first fast European line, the Paris–Lyon TGV, in 1981.

57

THE WORLD'S GREATEST RAIL ROUTES

BACKGROUND: Great Southern's "Indian Pacific" route passes through some of the world's most isolated country. Not far from the longest piece of straight track—478 km of unbending rail line on the Nullarbor Plain, Western Australia—a sole marsupial is the only local "trainspotter" for many miles around.

Image courtesy of Great Southern Rail

Courtesy of the James Northfield Heritage Art Trust ©

Travel by-
TRANS-
AUSTRALIAN
RAILWAY

TO PERTH

-in Comfort ———— save Days-

ACROSS AUSTRALIA

PACIFIC

INDIAN PACIFIC

CENTER: Striking James Northfield poster from the 1930s promoting the Trans-Australian Railway (a name still coined today for the Indian Pacific). One of the most recognized commercial artists of his time, Northfield's play of light and color captured the magic of the Australian landscape. At almost 1,700 km and at a cost of £4 million, the railway fundamentally altered Australians' outlook toward the western side of their country and connected Perth—once the most isolated city on the planet—to the rest of the burgeoning young nation.

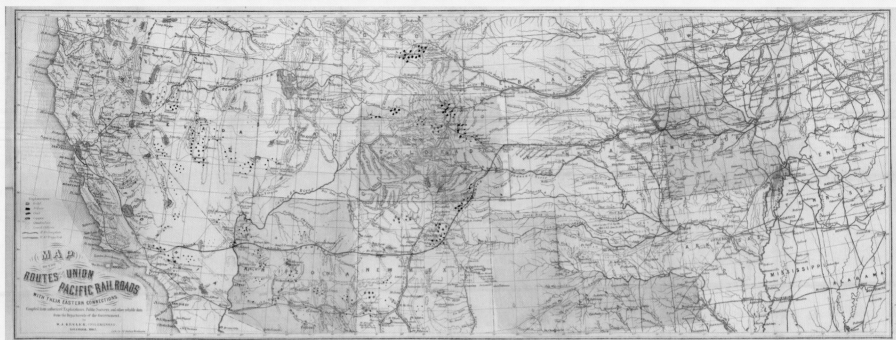

The first transcontinental railroads

It's easy in the fast-moving twenty-first century to forget just what a monumental achievement it was for the gigantic landmasses of what now form the USA and Canada to become unified countries and just how crucial was the role of the railroad in cementing those ties. The current extent of both countries evolved in a piecemeal fashion, but it was the absorption into the American Union during 1846 of the vast state of Texas; the annexing of Oregon in 1846; and the cessation of hostilities against Mexico two years later (when California, Nevada, and Utah, plus parts of Arizona, Colorado, New Mexico, and Wyoming, were added) that were to spur railroad construction on a scale completely dwarfing what was then happening in Europe.

An idea that called for an unprecedented cartographic challenge was finally agreed by federal charter in 1853; the Army Topographic Corps was charged with finding a practical and economic route across the empty plains and the impenetrable Sierra Nevada: a task so immense that it took almost ten years to complete.

On July 1, 1862, Abraham Lincoln signed "An act to aid in the construction of a railroad and telegraph line from the Missouri river to the Pacific ocean, and to secure to the government the use of the same for postal, military, and other purposes," (aka the Pacific Railroad Act), bringing into existence the Union Pacific Railroad company and permitting it and the Central Pacific Railroad of California to raise money for the unprecedented construction works.

The Union Pacific was to build westwards 1,749 km from the town of Council Bluffs, Omaha, while the Central Pacific was to lay 1,110 km of track eastwards beginning from Sacramento, California. The tasks involved countless thousands of army veterans, Irish immigrants, and Chinese laborers to complete the construction. Where material supply camps were established every forty or fifty kilometers along the route, shantytowns grew up, many of which later developed into fully fledged towns and cities with their own station on the line.

Though joined by the infamous ceremony at Promontory Summit, Utah, in 1869, crossing the full route from San Francisco to New York was not possible until 1876. Nonetheless this was an immense engineering achievement that changed the face and fortunes of the United States. Meanwhile, other trans–North American routes were already under way, including the Northern and the Canadian Pacific's.

ABOVE: William Keeler's 1867 map of the Union Pacific route.
FAR LEFT: Famous Union Pacific official 1869 opening-day poster claims the railroad runs from the Atlantic to the Pacific, though several changes of trains were necessary for this!
FACING TOP: The Northern Pacific was chartered in 1864 to serve the Northwest from Puget Sound to Lake Superior. Though it was completed in 1883, this 1900 map shows just how convoluted the route really was.
FACING FAR RIGHT: Celebrated 1881 painting The Driving of the Last Spike by Thomas Hill commemorates the great event. It is now on permanent display at the California State Railroad Museum, Sacramento.
FACING NEAR LEFT: How the Union Pacific was wound through the mountains of the Sierra Nevada.

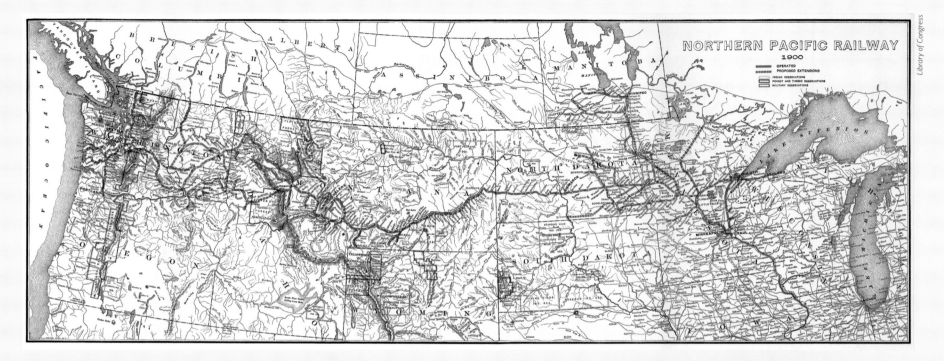

Library of Congress

"Finally the two sets of railroad tracks were joined and the continent united with elaborate ceremony at Promontory, Utah, on May 10, 1869. Travel time between America's east and west coasts was reduced from months to less than a week"

eyewitnesstohistory.com

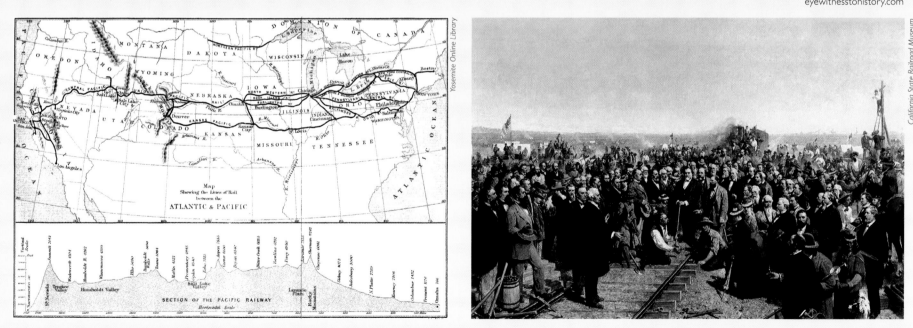

Yosemite Online Library

California State Railroad Museum

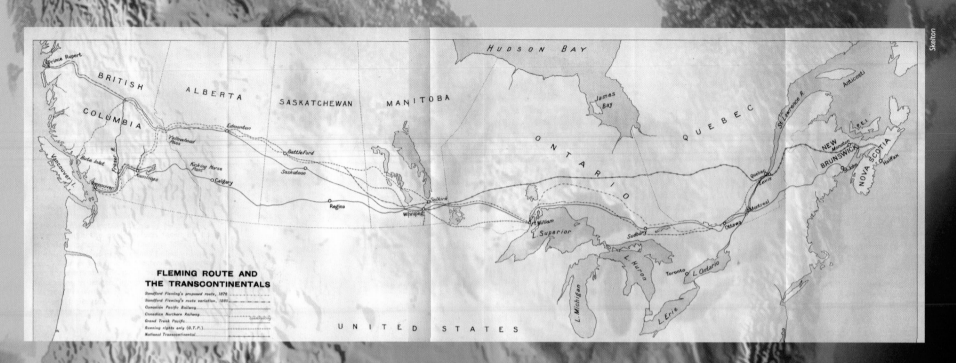

FLEMING ROUTE AND
THE TRANSCONTINENTALS

Sandford Fleming's proposed route, 1876 ....
Sandford Fleming's route variation, 1880 ....
Canadian Pacific Railway ....
Canadian Northern Railway ....
Grand Trunk Pacific ....
Running rights only (G.T.P.) ....
National Transcontinental ....

"The construction of a Canadian Pacific Railway is essential to the creation of a unified Canadian nation that will stretch across the continent"

Prime Minister Sir John A. Macdonald, 1871

MAP OF THE
CANADIAN PACIFIC RAILWAY
THE MINNEAPOLIS, ST. PAUL & SAULT STE. MARIE RAILWAY
THE DULUTH, SOUTH SHORE & ATLANTIC RAILWAY
THE SPOKANE INTERNATIONAL RAILWAY
NORTHERN ALBERTA RAILWAYS
AND CONNECTIONS

Canadian Pacific Railway
and
Steamship Lines

ABOVE: The famous Rocky Mountaineer passing Exshaw, Alberta. FACING TOP: All the possible routes considered for the Canadian transcontinental line in comparison to Sandford Fleming's 1876–80 proposals.

Canada coast to coast

As a condition for joining the Canadian Confederation, the massive state of British Columbia insisted on the building of links to the east. The government promised a rail connection in one decade (by 1871), but despite the benefits of opening up the interior, building a railroad through the Rockies meant traversing at least 1,600 km of virtually impenetrable mountainous wilderness. The government became embroiled in a financial scandal around land rights, causing the Conservative Party to be ousted in 1873. Instead, separate sections of new lines (i.e., joining Winnipeg to the existing network) were slowly begun by the new Liberal government of Alexander Mackenzie.

By 1878 the Conservatives were back and took a more vigorous approach. Bonds were sold and the Canadian Pacific Railway Company was incorporated (1881) and started work on pushing west from Ontario.

Respected engineer Sir Sandford Fleming had surveyed several northerly routes thru the Yellowhead Pass, but the CPR wanted a line closer to the US to discourage encroachments into Canada. This meant finding a far more

elusive route through the mountains. It was eventually found in 1881 by rail surveyor Albert Bowman Rogers. Despite steep gradients, floods, and some previous flawed reports, almost 700 km of track was laid by 1882, a branch reaching Thunder Bay in June. At the end of 1883, the tracks approached the Rocky Mountain foothills.

As in the US, the navvies were mostly immigrants, some of whom rebelled (conditions were so bad for some that the government formally apologized to the Chinese in 2006).

By the time the Last Spike was driven at Craigellachie, BC, on November 7, 1885, it had become the world's longest railway. Links at the eastern end soon gave branches to Toronto, Buffalo, and New York. The first transcontinental passenger train left Montreal June 28, 1886, arriving six days later at Port Moody. (Vancouver—originally known as Gastown—was reached by the tracks in 1887.)

More acquisitions and construction in the east enabled through services from the Atlantic to the Pacific and the CPR became both a profitable concern and the key driver of colonization inside Canada.

ACROSS CANADA

TOP: Based on a 1911 map, this 1930 revision shows the peak extent of the Canadian Pacific network in red (other companies' lines are in thinner black). ABOVE: Cover of CP guide with rail routes in white over red Canadian land.

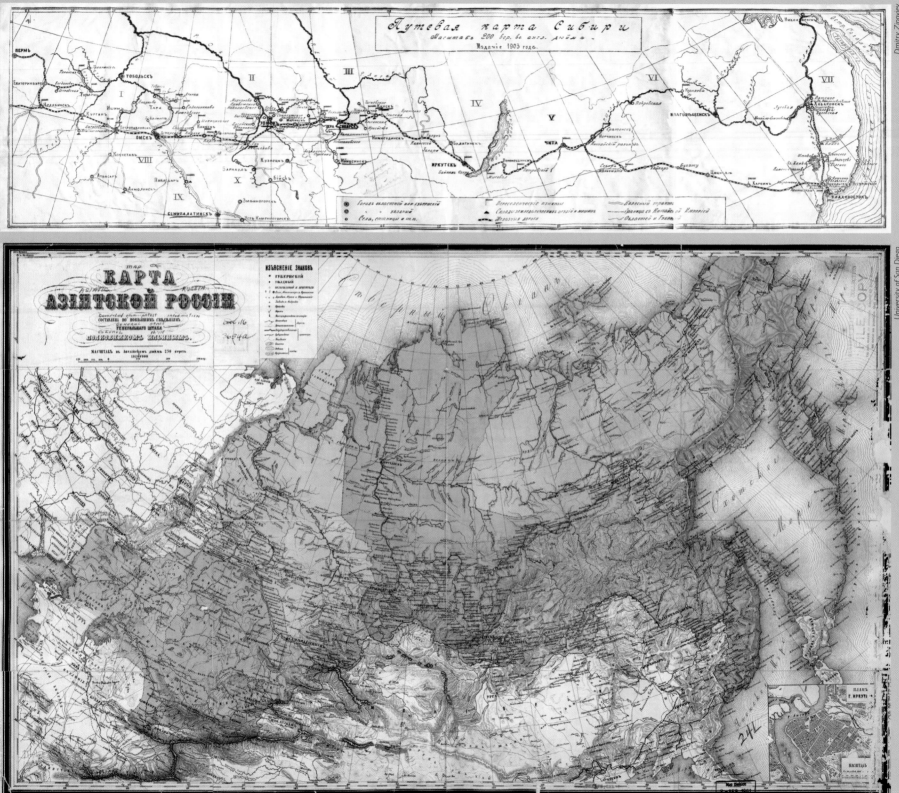

Путевая карта Сибири

Масштабъ 200 вер. въ англ. дюймѣ.

Изданіе 1903 года.

КАРТА
АЗІЯТСКОЙ РОССІИ

МАСШТАБЪ въ Англійскомъ дюймѣ 250 верстъ

ПЛАНЪ
Г. ИРКУТ

МАСШТАБЪ

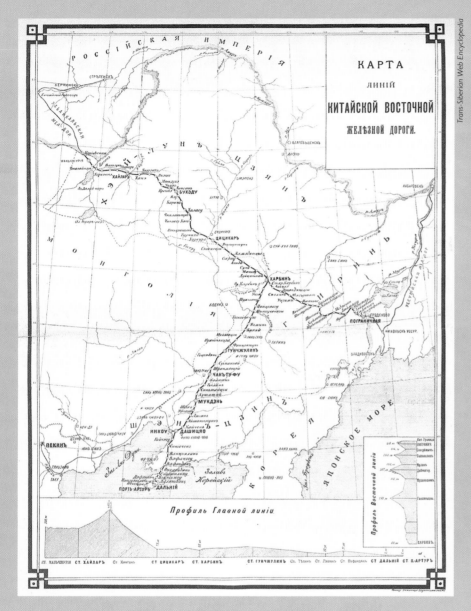

КАРТА ЛИНІЙ КИТАЙСКОЙ ВОСТОЧНОЙ ЖЕЛѢЗНОЙ ДОРОГИ.

FACING TOP: 1903 complete TS route.
FACING LOWER: 1912 all Russia map.
LEFT: 1903 Chinese Eastern and Trans-Manchurian sections.
PHOTO: Very early color photo of the Karma River bridge from 1912.
BELOW: Unusual 1916 dual diagram showing services in each direction on different days of the week.

The Trans-Siberian

КАРТА СЛѢДОВАНІЯ СКОРЫХЪ

Aspirations for an uninterrupted rail link across Europe and Asia go back to 1858, but it took 23 years of design and construction and over 1.4 billion rubles for the 9,259 km route (crossing seven time zones from Moscow to the Pacific port of Vladivostok) to be fully completed in 1903.

One of the biggest problems was how to get from Lake Baikal to Vladivostok: the easiest route meant crossing the northern Chinese province of Manchuria. An agreement was made to do this by building the Chinese Eastern Railway now known as the Trans-Manchurian route (with an 800 km "branch") that would split off at Harbin and run down to Dailin (an ice-free Pacific port). During the Russo-Japanese War, however, these sections were seized, so a new longer route inside Russian territory and avoiding Manchuria was necessary (and opened in 1916).

The Trans-Mongolian section (opened 1961) veers off at Ulan Ude, heading for Ulaanbaatar and Beijing, and the Baikal Amur section (not completed until 1991) leaves the Trans-Siberian (TS) at Taishet heading for Sovetskaya Gavan. The TS played a key role in Russia's history: it was used for military purposes and gave rise to countless settlements strung along the route, visible at night from space (page 1); it opened up Siberia, where other transport is useless during the long winters.

The world's longest continuous rail passenger journey, Kiev to Vladivostok (11,085 km), uses the TS for much of its route. A freight container can travel from Hamburg to Beijing in 15 days. About 30 percent of Russia's exports now utilize the line.

Orient mysteries

The name Orient Express was not one train but more of a brand that has been applied to a number of routes and destinations over the years. Historically traversing Europe from Paris to Constantinople (modern-day Istanbul) since 1883, it was originally operated by the luxurious trains of the French Compagnie Internationale des Wagons-Lits, and its reputation for style, decadence, and the occasional thriller have helped it to become one of the most infamous rail routes on the planet.

Direct trains to Turkey ended in 1976, so it ran (mostly) overnight from Paris to Venice under the name Venice-Simplon, the name emanating from the Simplon tunnel under the Alps (at almost 20 km the world's longest railway tunnel from 1922 until the opening of a Japanese one in 1988).

Due to the start of the TGV Est from Paris, the Venice-Simplon was curtailed in 2007, leaving only the backbone between Strasbourg and Vienna. In December 2009 even this section was halted—deleting the words "Orient Express" from timetables for the first time since the service officially appeared there in 1891. A private company still operates some tourist trains using the name, bringing back to life the elegance of the most romanticized train journeys in the world.

Mapping the route, with so many branches, countries crossed, national rail operators, destinations, and feeders has proved inexorably complex, and consequently, sadly, few good examples have survived.

Great Southern Rail

Ashworth collection

AUSTRALIAN RAIL JOURNEYS OF A LIFETIME

The Ghan Route

Indian Pacific Route

Timor Sea

Arafura Sea

Coral Sea

DARWIN

Mitchell Falls

Buccaneer Archipelago

Lake Argyle

Indian Ocean

Gulf of Carpentaria

Great Barrier Reef

Northern Territory

Ningaloo Reef

Western Australia

Queensland

Pacific Ocean

Alice Springs

Shark Bay

South Australia

• BRISBANE

Lake Eyre

New South Wales

Lake Disappointment

Lake Ballard

PERTH •

Great Australian Bight

ADELAIDE •

• SYDNEY

Southern Ocean

MELBOURNE •

Bass Strait

HOBART

THE GHAN

INDIAN PACIFIC

CROSS AUSTRALIA BY **TRANS-AUSTRALIAN RAILWAY**

The world's longest straight line

Mike Cooper-Difrancia

It is often said that it would be impossible to underestimate the radical shift in human inhabitation of the planet that the railways brought, but in the case of the vast inland tracts of our major continents this is more the case. During the nineteenth century, lacking even the most basic amenities, small settlements were established on vast, dusty open plains; in dense impenetrable jungles and forests; and high up in formerly uninhabited mountains . . . for the sole reason of building, maintaining, or servicing the new iron roads.

Nowhere more exemplifies this than the absolute wilderness through which the Trans-Australian Railway was forged in 1917. The desert was so pristine that between the 797 km marker (west of Ooldea) and the 1,275 km point (west of Loongana) exists the world's longest section of dead-straight railway track—a 478 km run without a single bend!

The motivation for building the line came in 1901, when the original six colonies were federated together into the Commonwealth of Australia, but Perth was so isolated that the pledge of a state-funded rail link was the major incentive for Western Australia to join. By 1909 almost 1,700 km had been surveyed, but construction across the desert eastwards from Kalgoorie and westwards from Port Augusta did not meet until 1917. At the time, steam locos needed regular watering posts, so seven stops (named after Australian prime ministers) were established for watering the locos and each grew into a little community—most of which are now abandoned. For example, the town of Cook (823 km west of Port Augusta) included a bush hospital, but since diesel trains no longer need water stops it is now a ghost town (just four inhabitants remain) in the middle of the deserted Nullarbor Plain. Though the Trans-Australian is primarily a major freight route, there are also two passenger services that operate along the line, the Indian Pacific and the Ghan.

National Library of Australia

WELCOME ABOARD 'THE INDIAN-PACIFIC'

RAILWAYS of AUSTRALIA

TOP LEFT: 2011 Indian Pacific map.
TOP RIGHT: 1930s poster.
ABOVE: 1980s dining car menu cover.

Paris to the Med

One of the greatest European railroad groups was the Compagnie des Chemins de Fer de Paris à Lyon et à la Méditerranée, the "PLM." Responsible for a route that first headed out from Paris toward the southeast in the 1860s, it grew to reach not only Lyon and the Alps but the port of Marseille. Taking over smaller lines and expanding operations to North Africa, the PLM's elegant trains brought exotic destinations within easy reach for chic sunseekers.

With the arrival of high-speed TGVs from Paris to Lyon in 1981, extended to the coast in 2001, this ultra-rapid route now enables passengers to get on a train in central Paris and get off by the Med in just three hours!

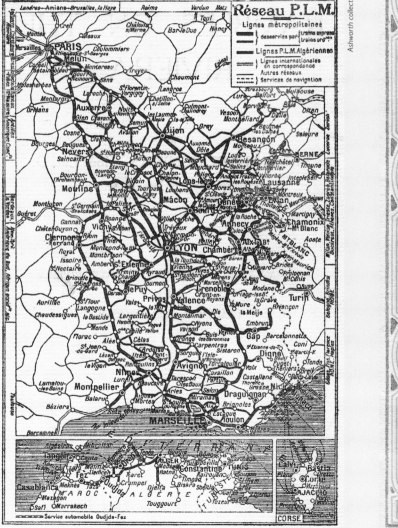

ABOVE LEFT: The impressive PLM network during 1915. ABOVE RIGHT: Intricate embossed cover from a 1915 PLM "Atlas" of Morocco, the gold-rimmed map somewhat exaggerating its proximity to France.

Satish Jayagopal, www.photo-capture.co.uk

The 2.3 km rail sea bridge connects
Rameshwaram on Pamban Island to
mainland India.

ATLAS

OF

WORLD RAILWAYS

TOP ROW: Map and travel guide covers from 1897 to 1923.

This atlas, the first of its kind, aims to present the *official* current national railroad map of every country where passenger rail service is operating at the time of the book's preparation (fall 2010).
Due to the inevitable technical difficulties of locating high-resolution images from such a wide variety of sources, where this has not been possible some "unofficial" versions have been included if necessary or appropriate, although this is made clear in the captions, which in this section of the book are numbered. Where space permits and historical material is available, network evolution or regional examples are given. Readers are asked to kindly make allowances for the quality of maps from countries where rail publicity and marketing are less advanced than those that come from other parts of the world.

Countries are listed by continent and then alphabetically.

For simplicity, Armenia, Azerbaijan, all of the Russian Federation, and all of Turkey are shown in Asia.

BOTTOM ROW: Map and travel guide covers from 1924 to 1937.

All images on this page taken from the Ashworth collection.

THE FUTURE GREAT RAILWAYS OF AFRICA

Reference
— Projected Railways
— Made or half-made Railways
— Water-routes navigable at all seasons

Scale 1:45,000,000 or 1 inch =710 Stan. Miles

AFRICA
Johnston

Map Division

AFRIKA
Maßstab 1: 35.000.000

Das Deutsche Reich
von Vergleich in Maßstab der Hauptkarte

The Library of Congress
DEC 3 & 1948
Division of Maps

STATION NAMES (in XML)
*3 Letter City Code
*Full City Name
*1 Letter Service
Code e.g.
CAI Cairo A
LXR Luxor A&C

ASSAULTING
* Stations can assault
adjacent stations along
their rail line
* Same city
stations can
assault each
other
*ABA-O connects
only with DSM-M

RAIL AFRICA
A (CAI–MYA) The Nile Liner   6
B (CAI–DKR) Gt Northern Exp   6
C (CAI–PSN) El Pharaoh Exp   2
D (CSB–ABJ) Sahara Express   5
E (LYN–TUN) L'Algérian
F (MDU–DKR) L'Continental
G (YND–DKR) Côte-d'Ivoire Exp 3
H (DJB–CPT) The Inlander
I (PTN–MYA) L'Equatorial
J (CPT–RBK) The Viper   3
K (RBK–DUR) East Coaster   6
L (CPT–LUB) Kalahari Express 5
M (CPT–PRA) Victoria Falls RR 8
N (CPT–PRA) Suid–Afrikaanse 4
O (TLR–ABA) Le Malgache   2
Ali (RBK) Rabak Stations   2
Nji (CPT) Capetown Stations

AFRO-TRAVEL
SAFR 1890

XML
AndrewB

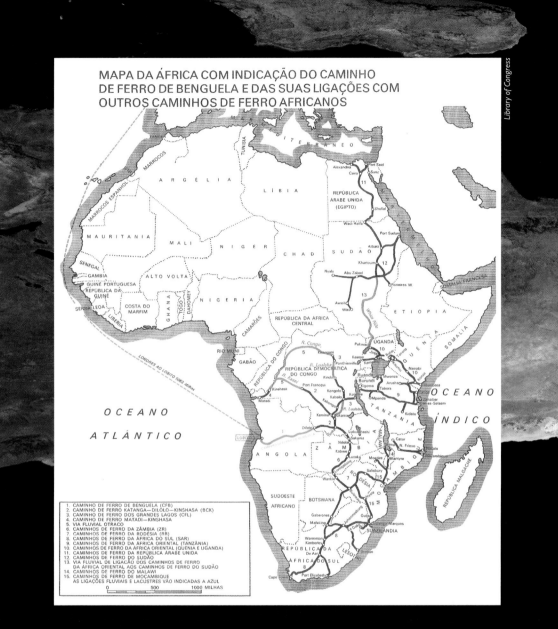

MAPA DA ÁFRICA COM INDICAÇÃO DO CAMINHO
DE FERRO DE BENGUELA E DAS SUAS LIGAÇÕES COM
OUTROS CAMINHOS DE FERRO AFRICANOS

Library of Congress

1. CAMINHO DE FERRO DE BENGUELA (CFB)
2. CAMINHO DE FERRO KATANGA—DILÔLO—KINSHASA (BCK)
3. CAMINHO DE FERRO DOS GRANDES LAGOS (CFL)
4. CAMINHO DE FERRO MATADI—KINSHASA
5. VIA FLUVIAL OTRACO
6. CAMINHOS DE FERRO DA ZÂMBIA (ZR)
7. CAMINHOS DE FERRO DA RODÉSIA (RR)
8. CAMINHOS DE FERRO DA ÁFRICA DO SUL (SAR)
9. CAMINHOS DE FERRO DA ÁFRICA ORIENTAL (TANZÂNIA)
10. CAMINHOS DE FERRO DA ÁFRICA ORIENTAL (QUÊNIA E UGANDA)
11. CAMINHOS DE FERRO DA REPÚBLICA ÁRABE UNIDA
12. CAMINHOS DE FERRO DO SUDÃO
13. VIA FLUVIAL DE LIGAÇÃO DOS CAMINHOS DE FERRO
    DA ÁFRICA ORIENTAL AOS CAMINHOS DE FERRO DO SUDÃO
14. CAMINHO DE FERRO DO MALAWI
15. CAMINHOS DE FERRO DE MOÇAMBIQUE
AS LIGAÇÕES FLUVIAIS E LACUSTRES VÃO INDICADAS A AZUL

0   500   1000 MILHAS

FACING CENTER: 1915 proposals for future African railroads.
FACING LOWER LEFT: 1909 plan.
FACING LOWER RIGHT: Andrew B's Rail Africa board game, set in 2018.

AFRICA
The least connected continent

CENTER: 1974 Pan-African proposals from the Angola-based Benguela Railway company (now known as the Caminho de Ferro de Benguela).

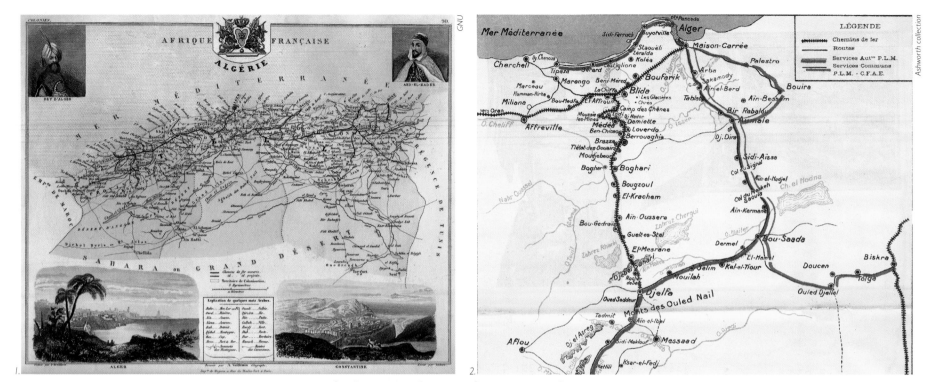

Algeria, Angola

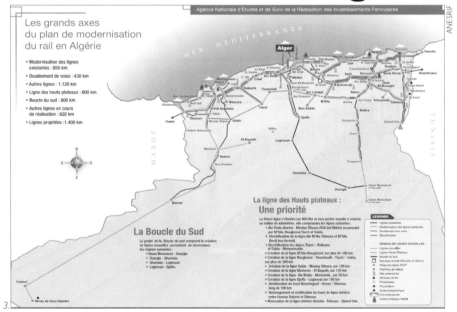

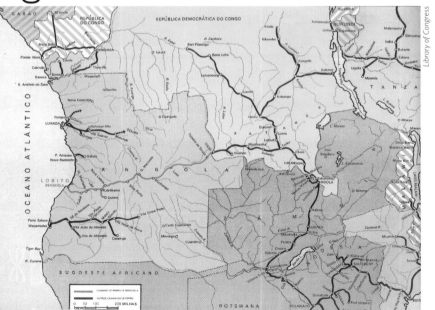

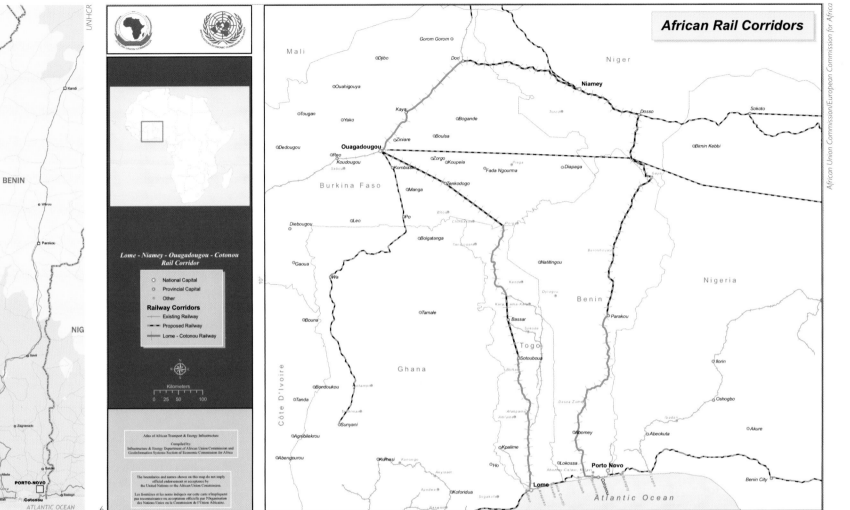

African Rail Corridors

Benin, Botswana, Burkina Faso

1: 1870s Algeria.
2: Northern Algeria transit in 1928.
3: Algeria's rail plans for 2012.
4: Angola's Bengeula Railway in 1975.
5: Detail from 2010 UN map of Benin.
6: UN/EU plans for West African rail routes via Benin and Burkina Faso.
7: Botswana's current rail lines.
8: 2010 unofficial map of Burkina Faso.

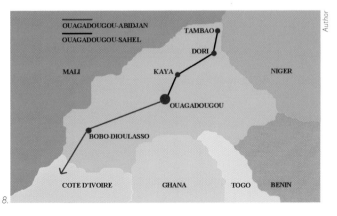

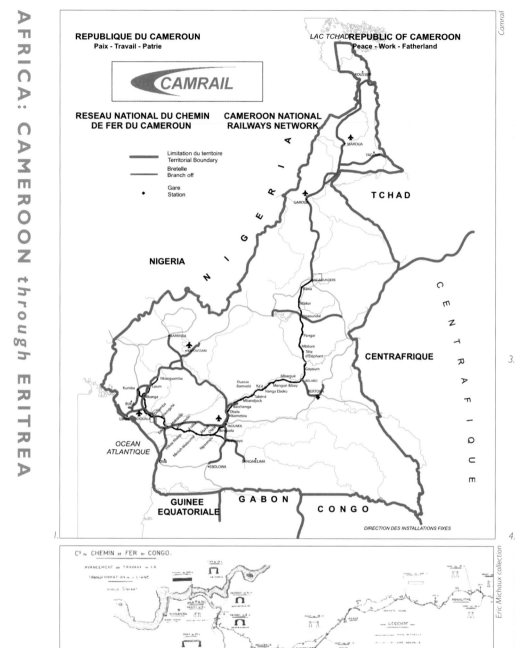

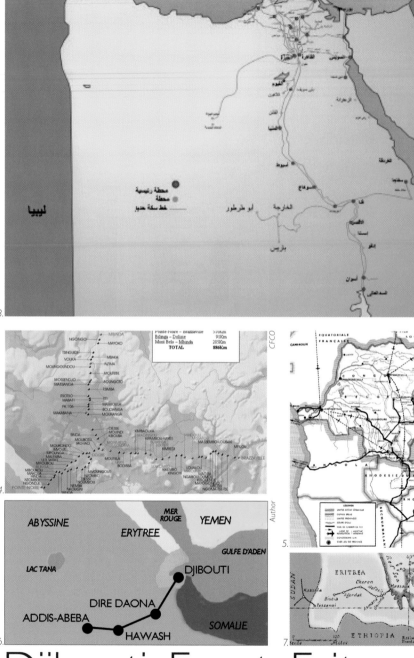

Cameroon, the Congos, Djibouti, Egypt, Eritrea

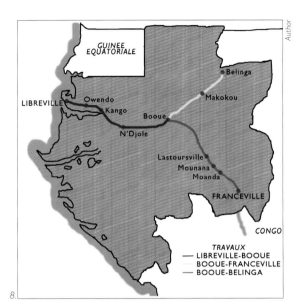

8.

1: 2005 Camrail network in Cameroon.
2: The Congo shown on a 1930 map.
3: The 2010 Egyptian rail network.
4: 2010 map of the CFCO network in the Democratic Republic of Congo.
5: The Belgian Congo, 1977.
6: Unofficial 2010 map of the rail routes in Djibouti.
7: Eritrea railways, date unknown.
8: Gabon's rail upgrade plan shown on an unofficial 2010 map.
9: 2010 SETRAG map of Gabon.
10: Unofficial Ghana network in 1995.
11: Ghana's 2010 reconstruction plan.
12: 2010 unofficial Guinea rail map.
13: Unofficial Côte d'Ivoire map, 2009.
14: Kenya and its neighbors were once united by the East African Railways and Harbours Board, seen here on an historic map from circa 1966.

9.

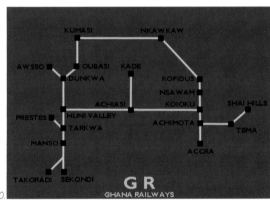

10.

11.

Gabon, Ghana, Guinea, Ivory Coast, Kenya

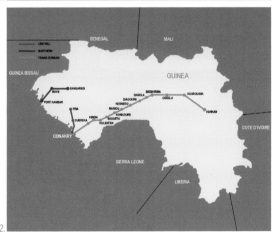

12.

13.

14.

Author

Great Socialist Peoples Libyan Arab Jamahiriya Railways Board

Dr. James A. Jones

1.

2.

5.

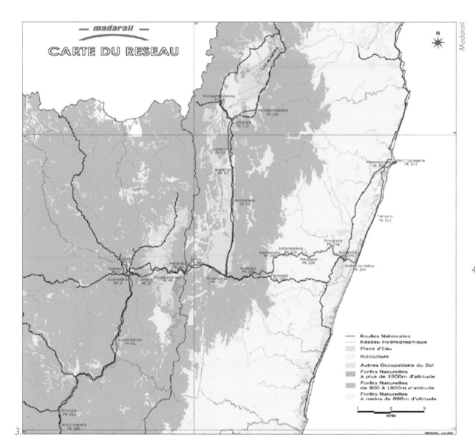

Madarail

3.

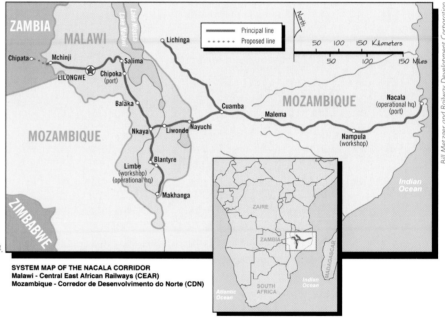

Bill Metzger and Railway Development Corporation

4.

SYSTEM MAP OF THE NACALA CORRIDOR
Malawi - Central East African Railways (CEAR)
Mozambique - Corredor de Desenvolvimento do Norte (CDN)

1: 2009 unofficial Liberia rail line map.
2: Libya closed its railroads in 1965 but is building this 3,170 km network.
3: Madagascar's Madarail in 2010.
4: 2010 map shows Malawi's connection to Mozambique via CEAR.
5: 2010 map shows Mali is served only by the Dakar-Niger Railway.

Liberia, Libya, Madagascar, Malawi, Mali

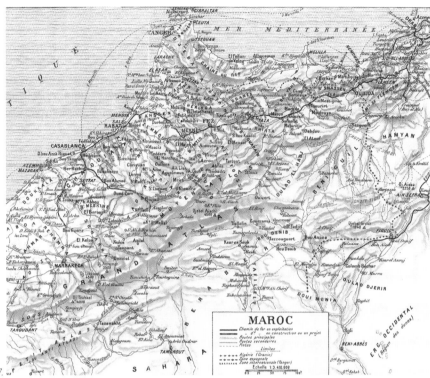

Morocco

6 & 7: Cover and map from 1930s
guide to Moroccan railways.
8: Morocco's plan for high-speed lines.

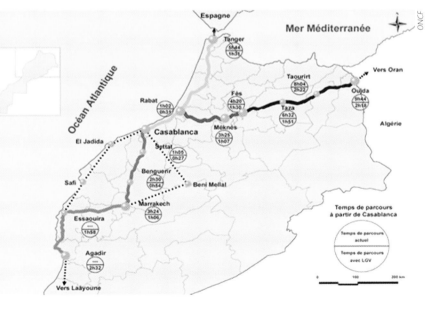

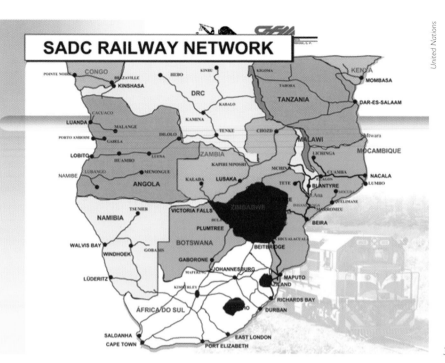

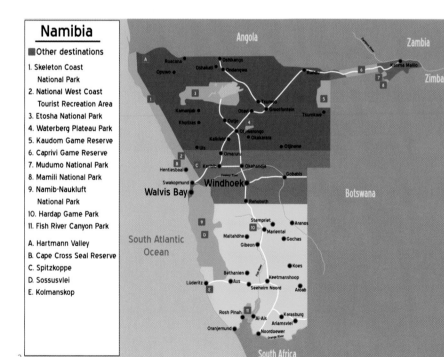

1: 2010 SADC map of Mozambique and nearby countries' lines.

2: Unofficial map of Namibia's current railway networks, 2010.

3: Unofficial 2010 Nigeria rail map.

4: Senegal services are mainly formed by the Dakar-Niger Railway, as seen on a 2010 map.

5: Unofficial 2010 Sudan rail map.

Mozambique, Namibia, Nigeria, Senegal, Sudan

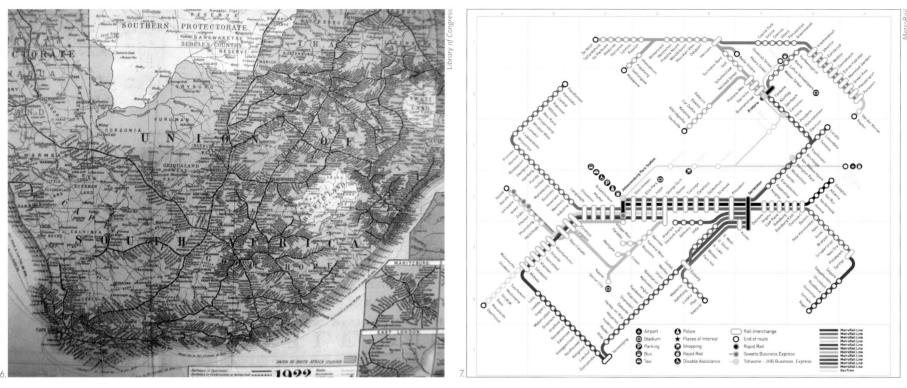

6: Detail from a 1922 southern Africa map when lines were at their zenith.
7: 2010 MetroRail suburban services in Gauteng, South Africa's most populous province.
8: 2009 map of the major intercity train routes of southern Africa as used by the freight carrier Spoornet.
9: From a 2010 brochure of the new Gautrain high-speed line, which will run between Pretoria and Johannesburg.
10: Beautifully illustrated 2010 map of the famous "Blue Train" scenic routes.

South Africa

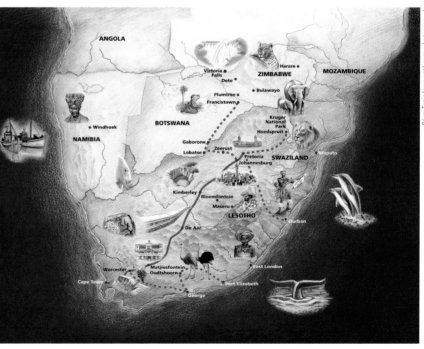

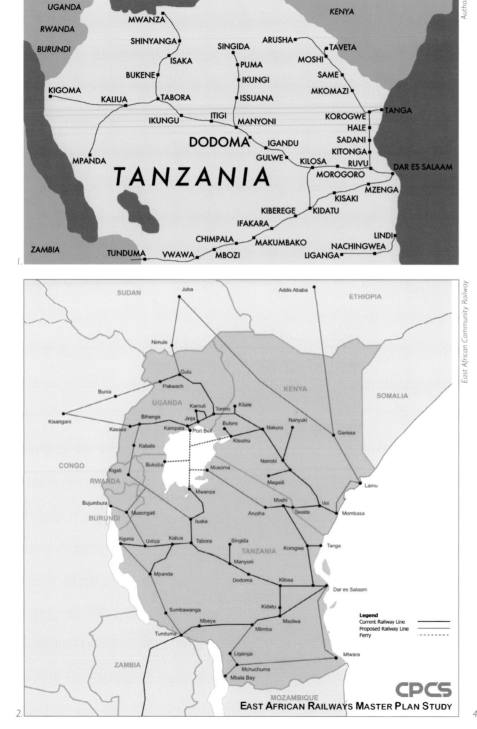

Author

East African Community Railway

Library of Congress

Legend
Current Railway Line
Proposed Railway Line
Ferry

CPCS

EAST AFRICAN RAILWAYS MASTER PLAN STUDY

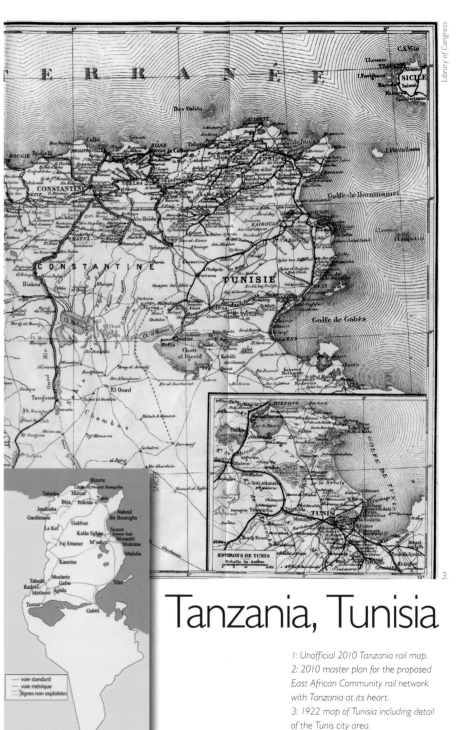

voie standard
voie métrique
lignes non exploitées

Tanzania, Tunisia

1: Unofficial 2010 Tanzania rail map.
2: 2010 master plan for the proposed East African Community rail network with Tanzania at its heart.
3: 1922 map of Tunisia including detail of the Tunis city area.
4: 2010 SNCFT Tunisia network map.

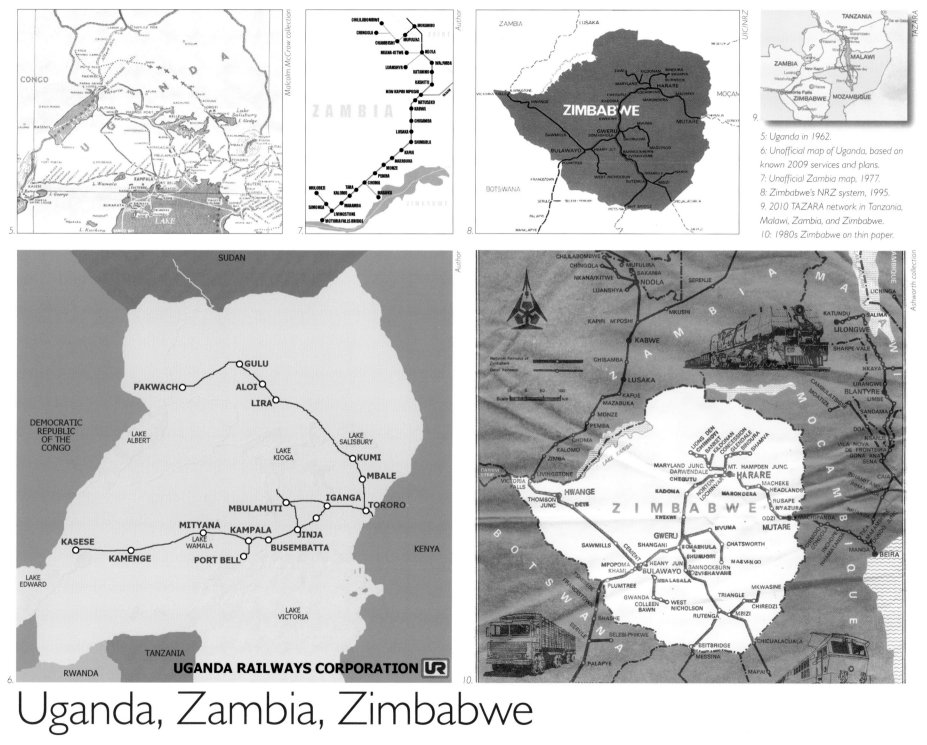

Malcolm McCrow collection

Author

UIC/NRZ

TAZARA

Author

Ashworth collection

5: Uganda in 1962.

6: Unofficial map of Uganda, based on known 2009 services and plans.

7: Unofficial Zambia map, 1977.

8: Zimbabwe's NRZ system, 1995.

9. 2010 TAZARA network in Tanzania, Malawi, Zambia, and Zimbabwe.

10: 1980s Zimbabwe on thin paper.

UGANDA RAILWAYS CORPORATION UR

Uganda, Zambia, Zimbabwe

THE PAN-AMERICAN RAILWAY
Based on the Map prepared by the
PAN-AMERICAN R. R. COMMITTEE
and accompanying the Report of
CHARLES M. PEPPER, Commissioner.
SCALE 1 : 40,550,000
SCALE OF MILES

Pan-American Route, Main Trunk
Proposed Connections
Railways in Operation.
"   under Construction or Surveyed
"   Projected

Library of Congress

Map Division
APR 11 1927
Library of Congress

CENTER: Unsurprisingly, railroad development south of the United States of America was utterly dominated by the financial interests of colonial powers, hence this 1904 plan for a "Pan-American" railway.

NASA

FACING: A 1913 plan shows that much work on the Pan-American was started, but a decade later it was still incomplete, and though raised again in 1925, the Depression and other financial woes finished the idea off.

MAP
SHOWING
RAILROADS
IN·OPERATION·
AND·UNDER·CONSTRUCTION·
IN
LATIN AMERICA
·PREPARED·BY·THE·
PAN·AMERICAN·UNION
JOHN BARRETT   FRANCISCO J. YÁNES
Director General   Assistant Director
1913

RAILROADS IN OPERATION
RAILROADS UNDER CONSTRUCTION

Enterprise, excess, and extermination

THE AMERICAs

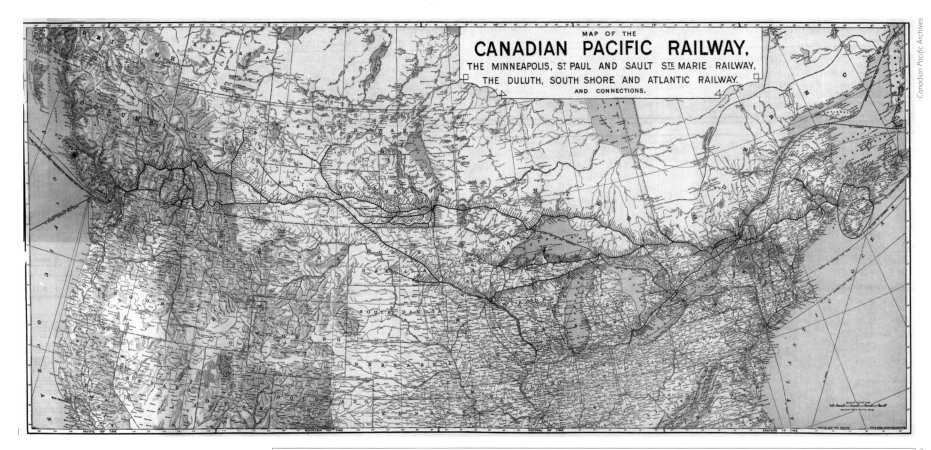

1: 1893 Poole Bros. map of the
Canadian Pacific Railway.
2: The CPR portrayed itself as
circumnavigating the world.
3: David Marlor's unofficial 2009 full
Canada-wide schematic of passenger
rail services. Given that Canada is the
world's second biggest country, and
the large number of lines it once had,
it is very sad to see how few passenger
services remain open today.
4: 2010 ViaRail hybrid map using
geographic backdrop with schematic
plan of lines overlaid.
5: 2010 ViaRail services schematic of
key cities served.

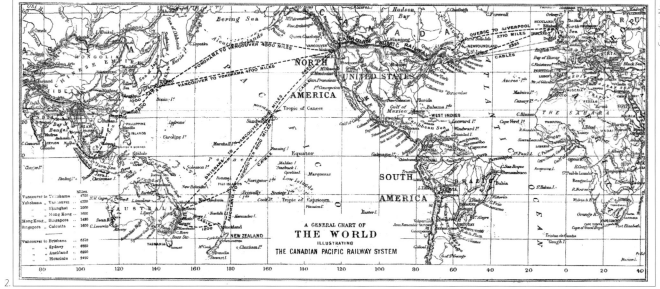

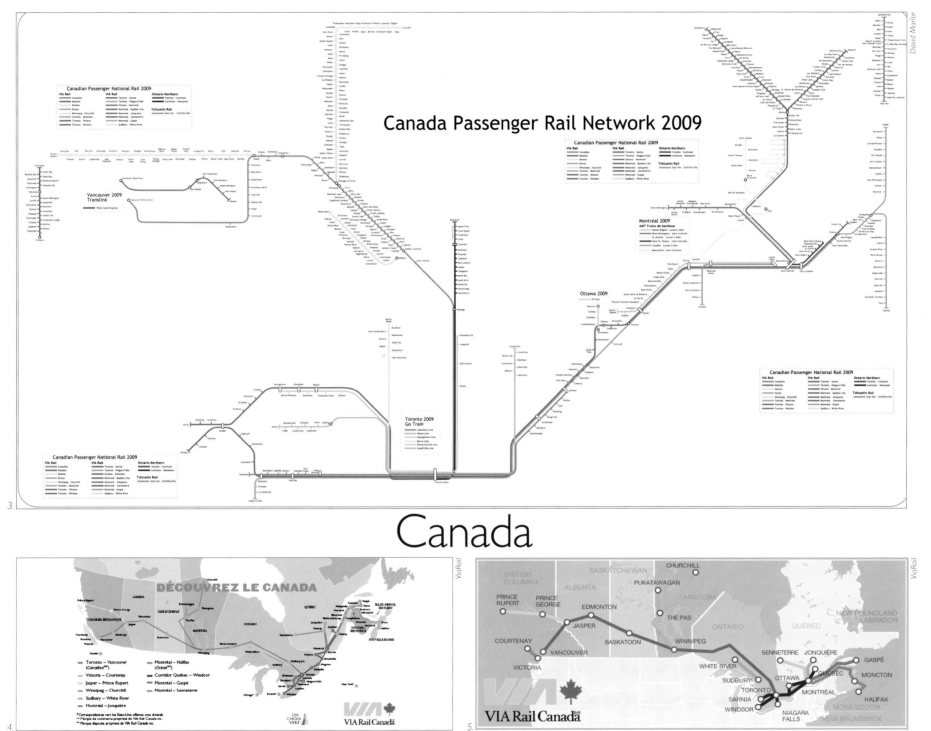

Canada

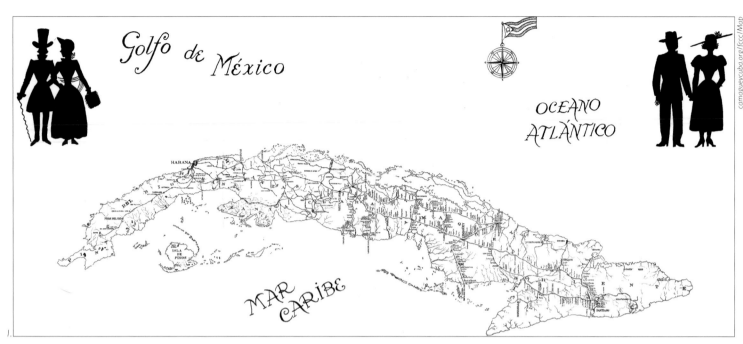

Golfo de México

OCEANO ATLÁNTICO

HABANA

DEL

ISLA DE PINOS

MAR CARIBE

SANTIAGO

camagueycuba.org/fccl/Map

1: Cuba's rail network in the 1950s.
2: The refurbished Heredia–San Jose railway is the only one in Costa Rica.
3: Guatemala's remaining rail line was suspended in 2007.
4: Mexico railways and connections to the USA running and planned in 1881.
5: Ferromexico's tracks in 1994. Many lines were by then in a relatively poor condition and subsequently all Mexican railways closed to passenger traffic.
6: While some freight lines stayed open (notably the Kansas City Southern de Mexico): Mexico's sole heavy passenger rail service, the Ferrocarriles Suburbanos (a recently reopened suburban route operating out of Mexico City), is all that is left of the country's rail heritage.
7: Government proposals for a rail revival across many parts of Mexico: proposed to be operational by 2012.
8: San Juan's heavy-rail commuter route TrenUrbano, opened in 2004.

Costa Rica, Cuba, Guatemala

RUTA DEL TREN
PAVAS - U. LATINA
Estación Atlántico - Heredia

Estación Heredia
Miraflores
Santa Rosa
Cuatro Reinas
Tivolyes
Villa Esperanza
Salle
Contraloria
Jack's
Atlántico
Cementerio
Pacifico
Museo
Plaza Viquez
Fresno Curridabat
UCR
U. Latina

Xavier Morera/Instituto Costaricense de Ferrocarriles

MEXICO

Cuba
Mexico
Guatemala
Caribbean Sea
Pacific Ocean
Colombia
400 Miles

Active Line
Inactive Line

Puerto Barrios (port)
Puerto Santo Tomás (port)
Morales
Quiriguá
Gualán
Zacapa
HONDURAS

GUATEMALA

El Rancho
El Progreso
Chiquimula

Tecún Umán
FCCM

Rio Bravo

Angulatú
San Jerónimo

EL SALVADOR

Champerico

GUATEMALA
(Administrative HQ and workshop)

Escuintla

FENDESAL

San Jose   Puerto Quetzal

Ahuachapan

North

50   100   150 Kilometers

50   100   150 Miles

Pacific Ocean

Acajutla   SAN SALVADOR

Map by Bill Metzger

Bill Metzger and Railway Development Corporation

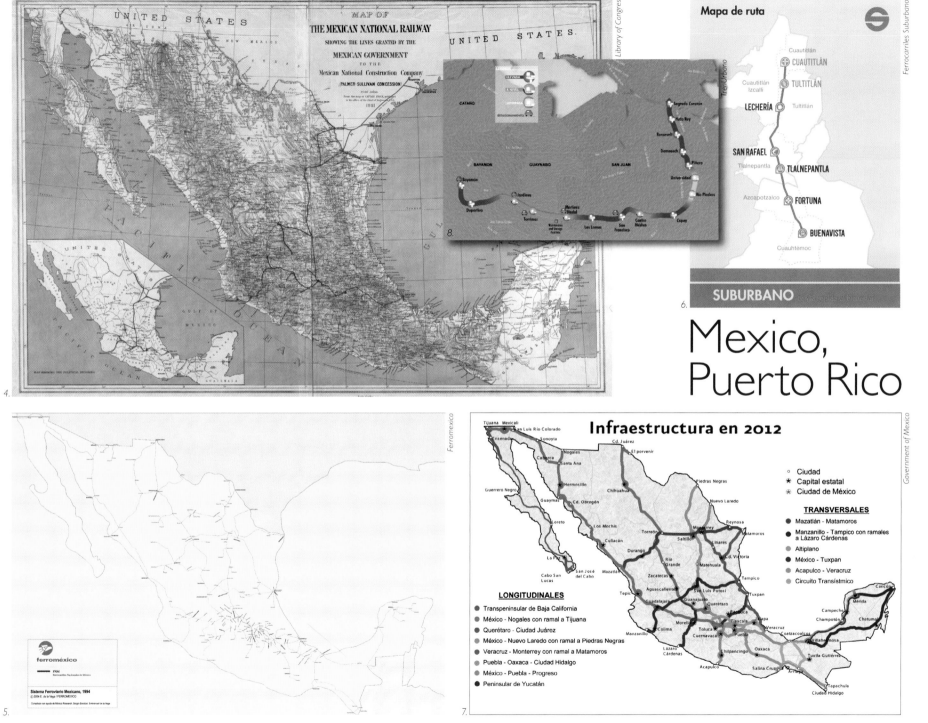

Library of Congress

Ferrocarriles Suburbanos

Mapa de ruta

Tren Urbano

Cuautitlán

⊕ CUAUTITLÁN

⊕ TULTITLÁN

Cuautitlán Izcalli

Tultitlán

LECHERÍA

SAN RAFAEL

Tlalnepantla

⊕ TLALNEPANTLA

Azcapotzalco

⊕ FORTUNA

⊕ BUENAVISTA

Cuauhtémoc

SUBURBANO

6.

Mexico, Puerto Rico

4.

8.

Ferromexico

ferroméxico

PNM
Ferrocarriles Nacionales de México

Sistema Ferroviario Mexicano, 1994

5.

Government of Mexico

Infraestructura en 2012

○ Ciudad
✱ Capital estatal
⊛ Ciudad de México

TRANSVERSALES

● Mazatlán - Matamoros
● Manzanillo - Tampico con ramales a Lázaro Cárdenas
● Altiplano
● México - Tuxpan
● Acapulco - Veracruz
● Circuito Transístmico

LONGITUDINALES

● Transpeninsular de Baja California
● México - Nogales con ramal a Tijuana
● Querétaro - Ciudad Juárez
● México - Nuevo Laredo con ramal a Piedras Negras
● Veracruz - Monterrey con ramal a Matamoros
● Puebla - Oaxaca - Ciudad Hidalgo
● México - Puebla - Progreso
● Peninsular de Yucatán

7.

89

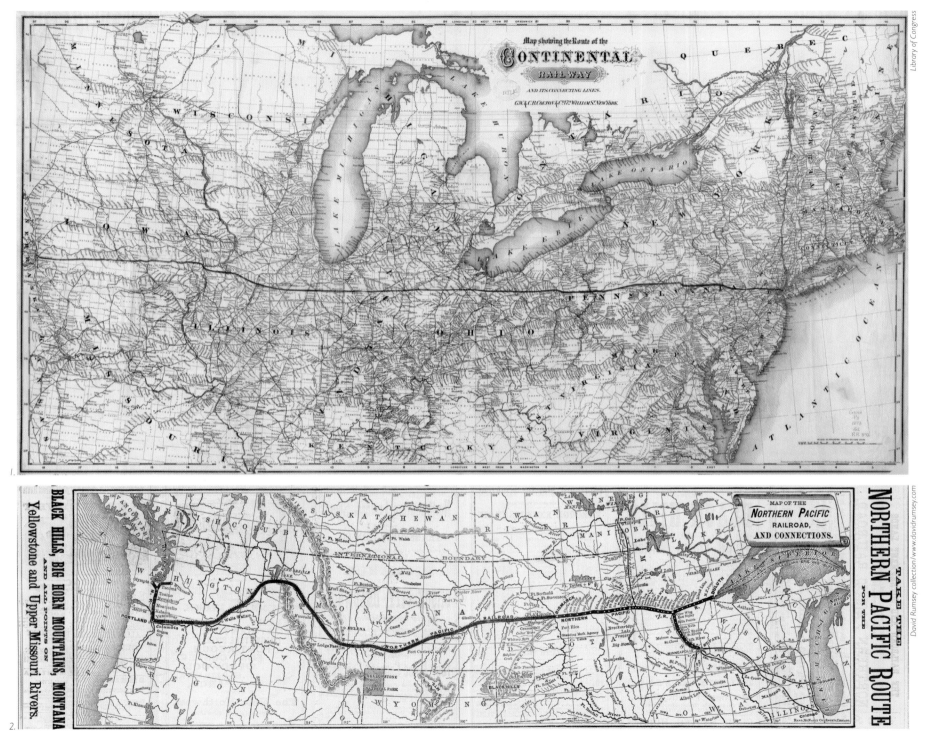

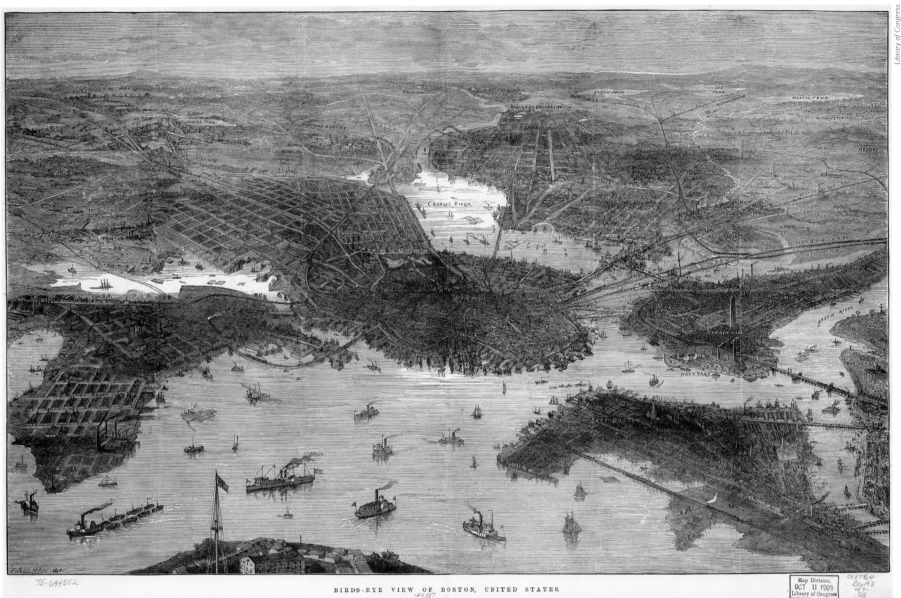

BIRDS-EYE VIEW OF BOSTON, UNITED STATES.

1: An 1873 plan of existing US lines and a dreamed-of "Continental" route.
2: 1879 Rand McNally map. Though opened in parts from 1864, the semi transcontinental Northern Pacific was only fully ready by 1888.

USA

3: Stunningly detailed and quasi–geographically accurate 1870s bird's-eye view of Boston Harbor showing the many railways at that point emanating from the city and their paths out into Massachusetts.

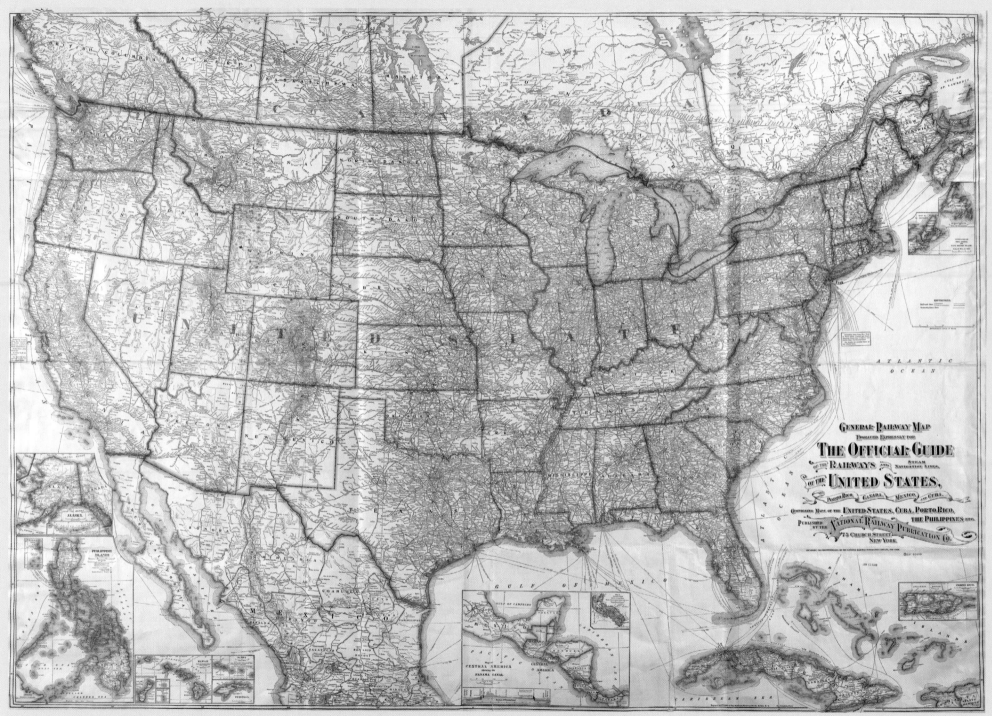

GENERAL RAILWAY MAP
ENGRAVED EXPRESSLY FOR
THE OFFICIAL GUIDE
OF THE RAILWAYS AND STEAM NAVIGATION LINES,
OF THE **UNITED STATES,**
PORTO RICO, CANADA, MEXICO, AND CUBA.

COMPRISING MAPS OF THE UNITED STATES, CUBA, PORTO RICO,
THE PHILIPPINES ETC.
PUBLISHED BY THE NATIONAL RAILWAY PUBLICATION CO.
75 CHURCH STREET,
NEW YORK.

An outstanding representation of the world's largest railroad network: the United States of America at its 408,777 km zenith in 1918.

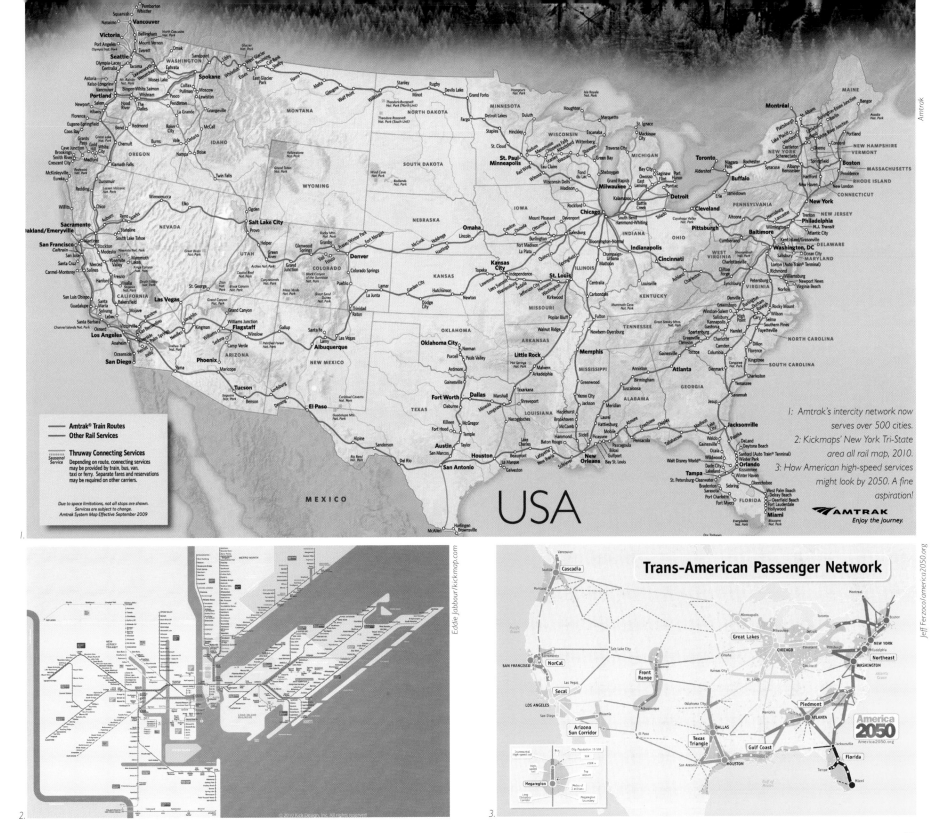

USA

1. Amtrak's intercity network now serves over 500 cities.
2. Kickmaps' New York Tri-State area all rail map, 2010.
3. How American high-speed services might look by 2050. A fine aspiration!

Amtrak Train Routes
Other Rail Services

Thruway Connecting Services
Seasonal Service
Depending on route, connecting services may be provided by train, bus, van, taxi or ferry. Separate fares and reservations may be required on other carriers.

Due to space limitations, not all stops are shown. Services are subject to change. Amtrak System Map Effective September 2009

AMTRAK
Enjoy the journey.

Trans-American Passenger Network

Cascadia
NorCal
Socal
Arizona Sun Corridor
Front Range
Great Lakes
Northeast
WASHINGTON
NEW YORK
Piedmont
ATLANTA
Texas Triangle
Gulf Coast
DALLAS
HOUSTON
Florida

America 2050
America2050.org

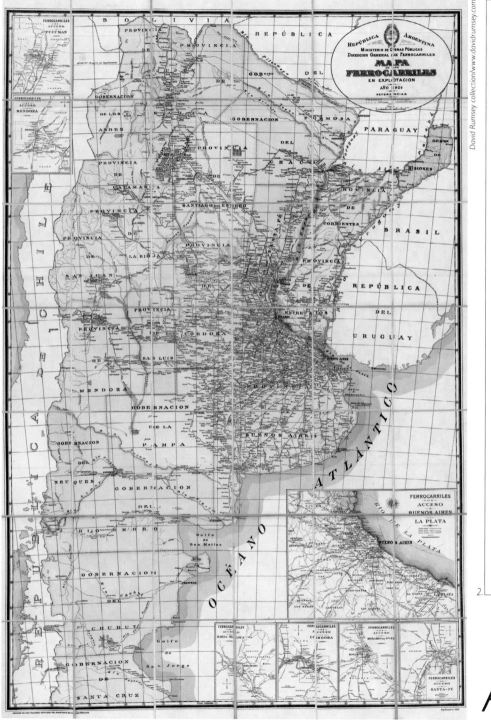

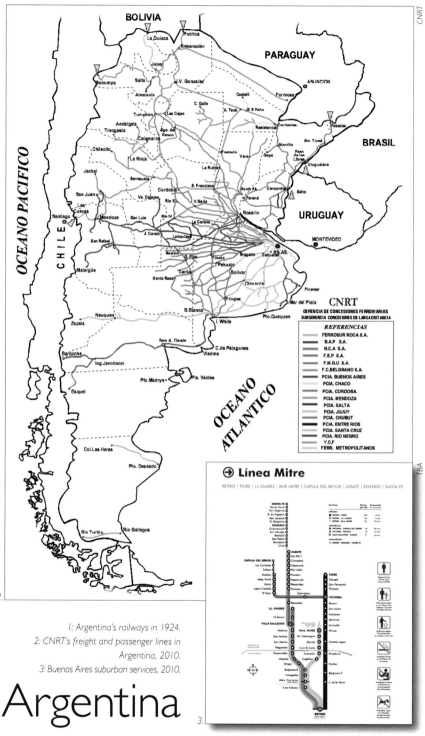

1: Argentina's railways in 1924.
2: CNRT's freight and passenger lines in Argentina, 2010.
3: Buenos Aires suburban services, 2010.

Argentina

NUESTRAS
RUTAS
NUESTROS
DESTINOS

4.

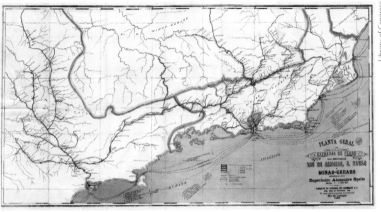

7.

4: Bolivia's one remaining rail line, run by Empresa Nacional de Ferrocarriles, on a colorful 2010 map.

5: Central Bolivia detail on 1913 map.

6: The Trans-Andean line that once crossed Bolivia from Peru to Argentina on a 1924 map.

7: One of Brazil's first lines in 1885.

8: 2010 map of Brazil's rail services. The privatization process was complete by 2007, breathing much-needed investment into the system after years of neglect by the old RFFSA. There are also now plans for a high-speed line between Rio de Janeiro and São Paulo.

5.

Bolivia, Brazil

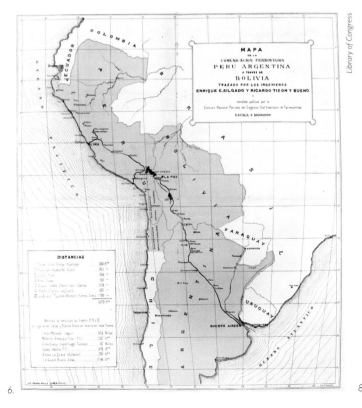

6.

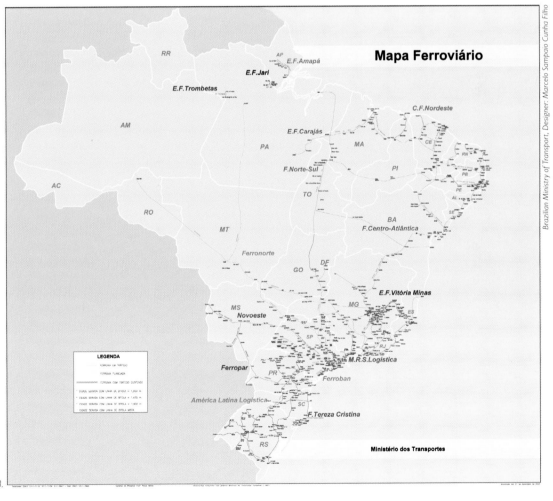

Mapa Ferroviário

Ministério dos Transportes

8.

Chile, Colombia, Ecuador

Richard Meyer/Norman B. Leventhal Map Center @ Boston Public Library

EFE

UIC/STF

FNC

EFE

1.

2.

3.

4.

5.

Panama, Peru, Trinidad, Uruguay, Venezuela

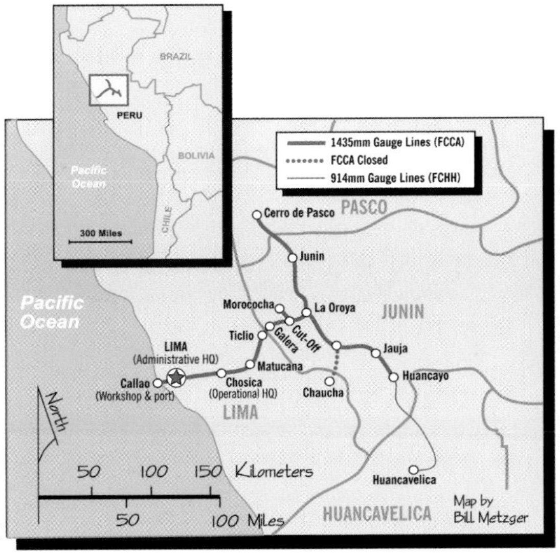

1: 1920s Chilean railroads.
2: Existing lines in Chile, 2010.
3: The FAC's Colombia northern line.
4: Colombia's lines (shown in black) on a 1980s STF map.
5: 2010. Ecuador's remaining train line.
6: In 1855 Panama's line was the first to traverse the American continent.
7. 2010 map of Peru's RRDC lines.
8: Peru's Machu Picchu train, 2010.
9: Plans for a new 98 km rail system in Trinidad called Trinitrain.
10: 2010 AFE rail lines in Uruguay.
11: Venezuela rail system, 2010.
12: IFE plans for Venezuela by 2030.

7.

Bill Metzger and Railroad Development Corporation

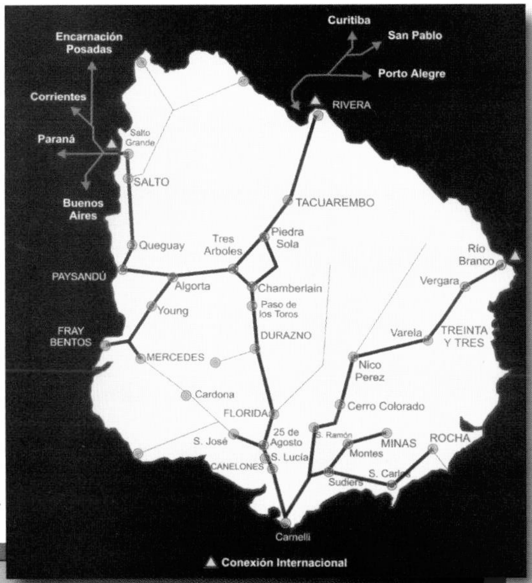

10.

AFE

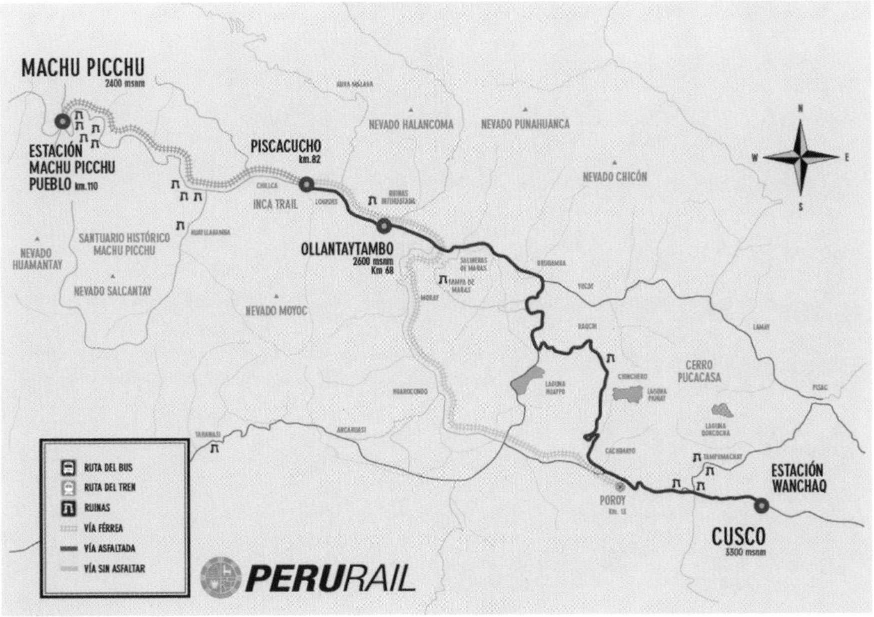

8.

Perurail

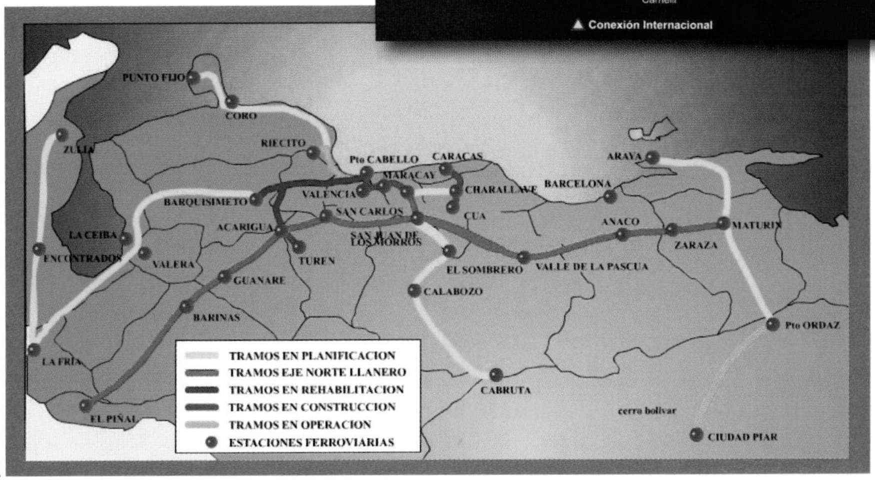

11.

IAFE

6.

GNU

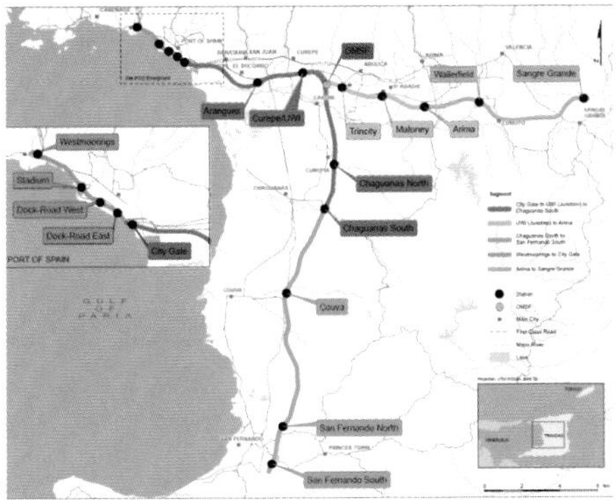

9.

Trinitrain

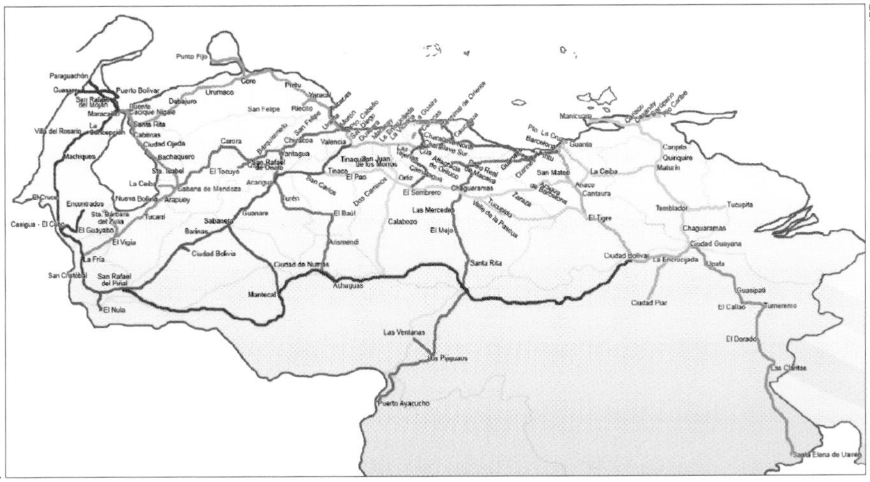

12.

IFE

97

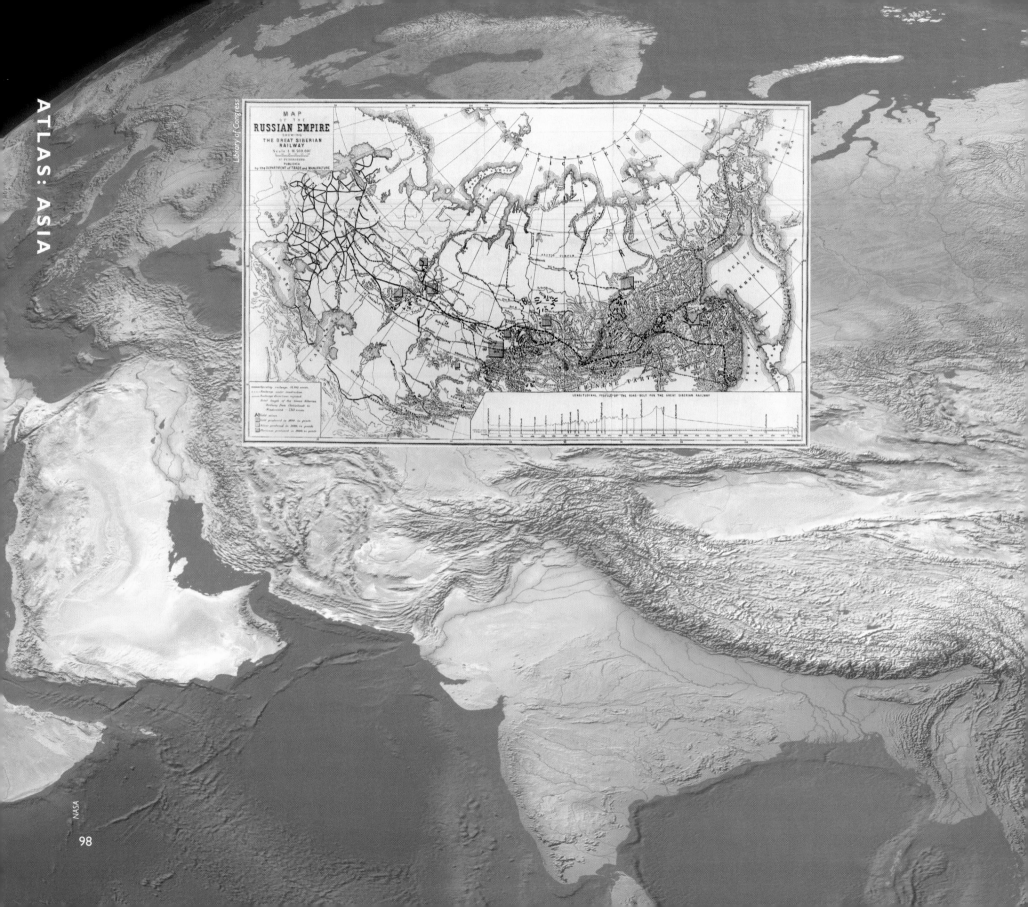

Library of Congress

MAP
OF THE
RUSSIAN EMPIRE
SHOWING
THE GREAT SIBERIAN
RAILWAY

NASA

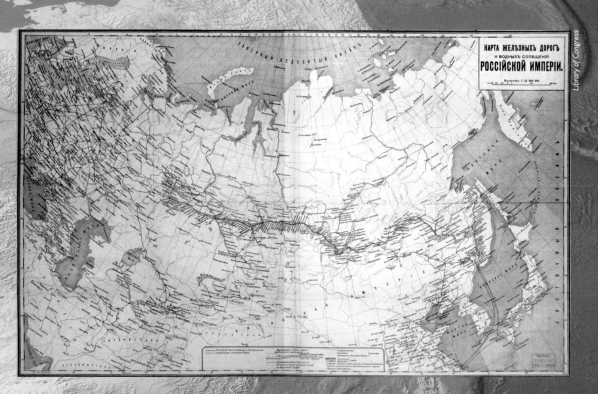

КАРТА ЖЕЛѢЗНЫХЪ ДОРОГЪ
И ВОДНЫХЪ СООБЩЕНІЙ
РОССІЙСКОЙ ИМПЕРІИ.

Library of Congress

A S I A
Tracking across the largest landmass

FACING: Railroad engineers have dreamed of crossing continents since before the technology made it possible, so what bigger challenge than the vast expanses of Asia? This 1890 map shows mineral deposits and plans for the longest railroad ever conceived.

CENTER: With tenacity and imperial wealth—not to mention heavy loss of life—the Trans-Siberian crossed seven time zones and united disparate lands into the world's largest nation. This 1954 Russian map makes the journey look easy—but it still takes two weeks!

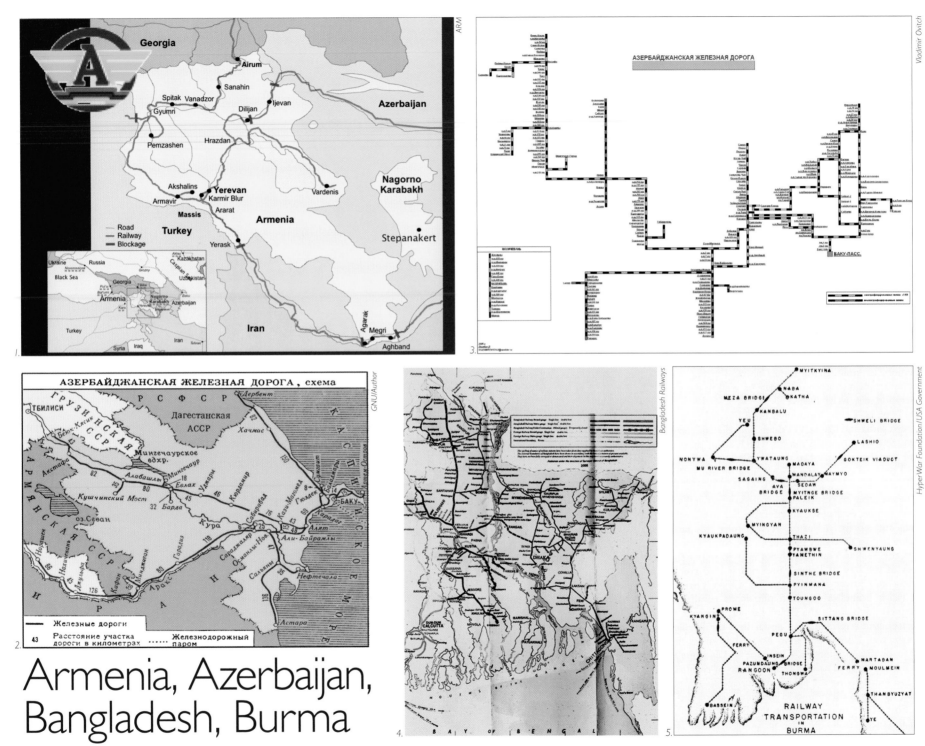

Armenia, Azerbaijan, Bangladesh, Burma

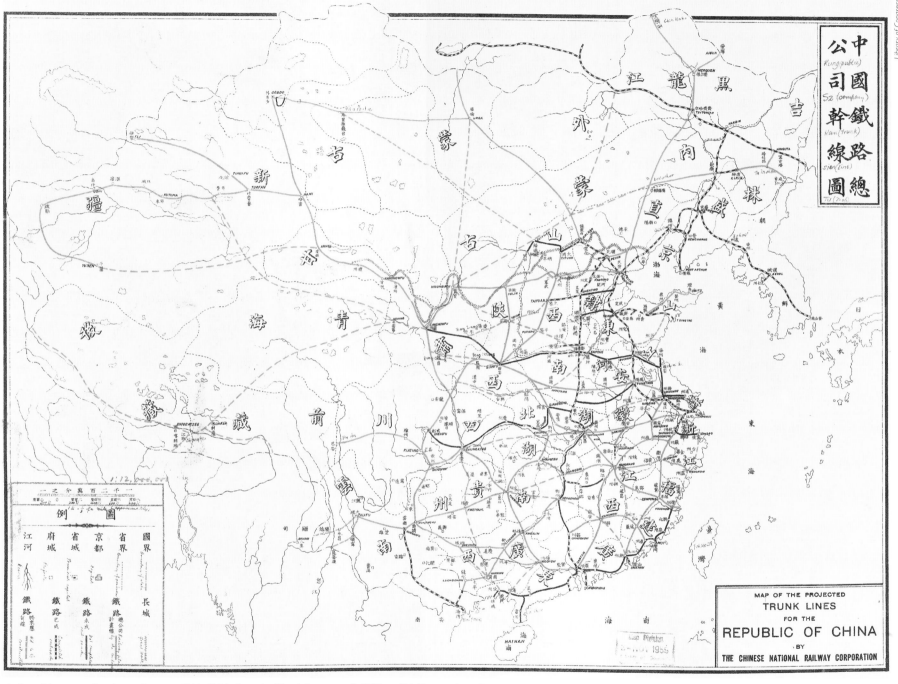

6.

1: Armenia's current railroad network.

2: 1940s Russian map of Azerbaijan and neighboring countries.

3: Unofficial schematic of Azerbaijan made during 2005 by Vladimir Ovich.

4: Official 2010 Bangladesh map.

5: 1940s unofficial Burma schematic.

6: A forward-thinking plan for a full Chinese network prepared in 1913.

China

101

1: Detail from 1917 Chinese plan for new lines in Manchuria.
2: 1935 American map showing what had been achieved in Manchuria.
3: Detail from the 1952 economic recovery plan showing proposed lines.
4: Official current Chinese government map including plans for future upgrades and new lines.
5: 2010 rail network in China.

China

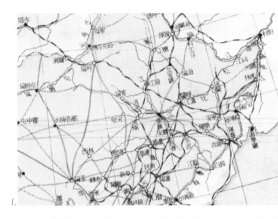

Library of Congress

1.

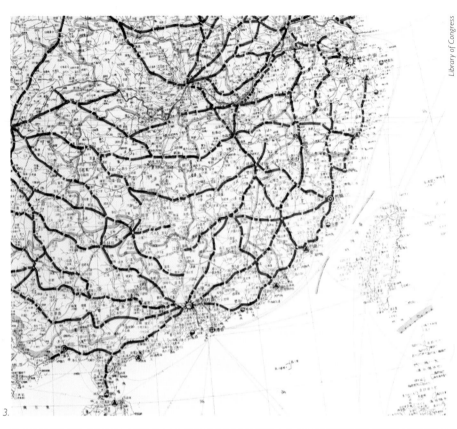

Library of Congress

3.

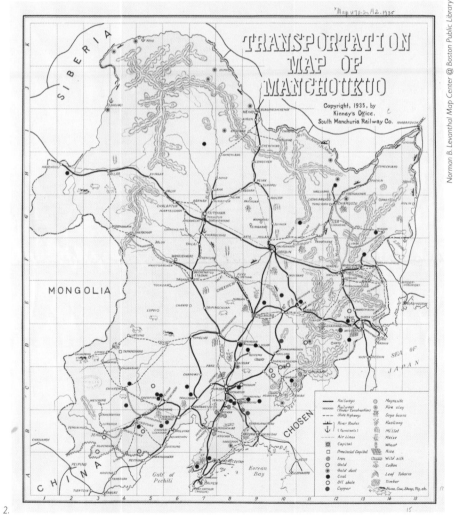

Norman B. Levanthal Map Center @ Boston Public Library

TRANSPORTATION MAP OF MANCHOUKUO

Copyright, 1935, by
Kinney's Office.
South Manchuria Railway Co.

2.

Ministry of Railways

铁路局管辖范围

4.

中国铁路营业线路

中国铁道出版社 2008年12月编制

图 例

国界、未定国界
省、自治区、直辖市界
双线铁路
单线铁路
双线电气化铁路
单线电气化铁路
窄轨铁路
铁道部所在地
铁路局(集团公司)所在地
主要车站
轮渡

南海诸岛

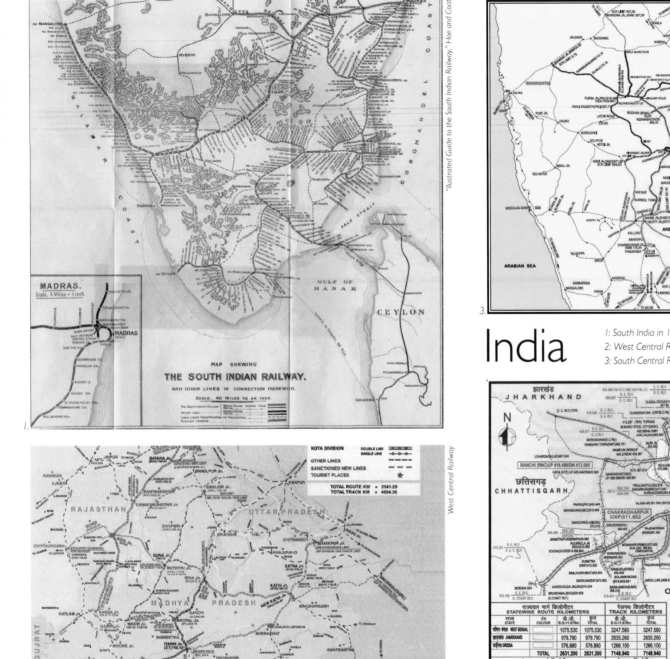

"Illustrated Guide to the South Indian Railway," Hoe and Coat

West Central Railway

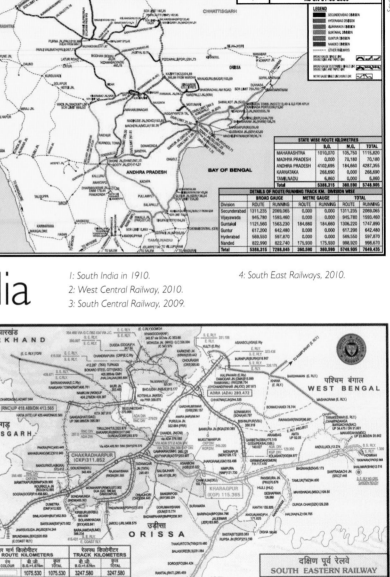

South Central Railway

South Eastern Railway

India

1: South India in 1910.

2: West Central Railway, 2010.

3: South Central Railway, 2009.

4: South East Railways, 2010.

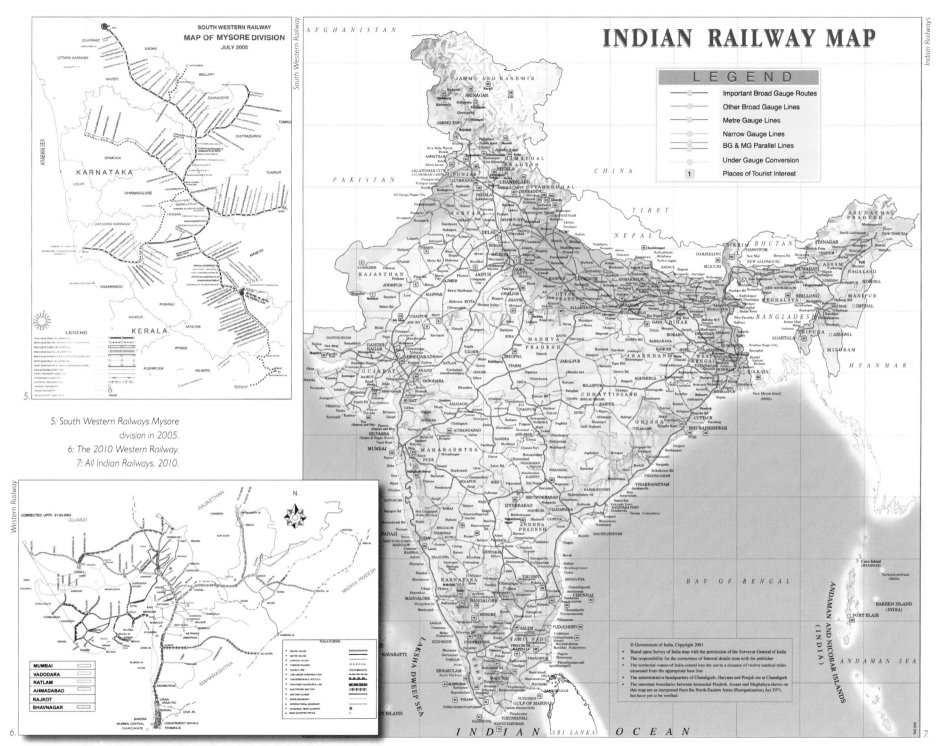

Indian Railways

South Western Railway

SOUTH WESTERN RAILWAY
MAP OF MYSORE DIVISION
JULY 2005

5: South Western Railways Mysore
division in 2005.
6: The 2010 Western Railway.
7: All Indian Railways, 2010.

Western Railway

CORRECTED UPTO 31-03-2003

INDIAN RAILWAY MAP

LEGEND

Important Broad Gauge Routes
Other Broad Gauge Lines
Metre Gauge Lines
Narrow Gauge Lines
BG & MG Parallel Lines
Under Gauge Conversion
Places of Tourist Interest

© Government of India, Copyright 2001
• Based upon Survey of India map with the permission of the Surveyor General of India
• The responsibility for the correctness of Internal details rests with the publisher
• The territorial waters of India extend into the sea to a distance of twelve nautical miles measured from the appropriate base line
• The administrative headquarters of Chandigarh, Haryana and Punjab are at Chandigarh
• The interstate boundaries between Arunachal Pradesh, Assam and Meghalaya shown on this map are as interpreted from the North-Eastern Areas (Reorganisation) Act 1971, but have yet to be verified.

Indonesia, Iran, Iraq, Israel

1: Eastern Java in the 1930s.
2: Current rail services on Java.
3: Iran rail lines in 1977.
4: Current and planned Iran rail.

5: Iraq's rail network (red) in 1930.
6: Hejaz pilgrims railway in the 1940s.
7: 1940s Palestine Railway services.
8: Israel's current rail network, 2010.

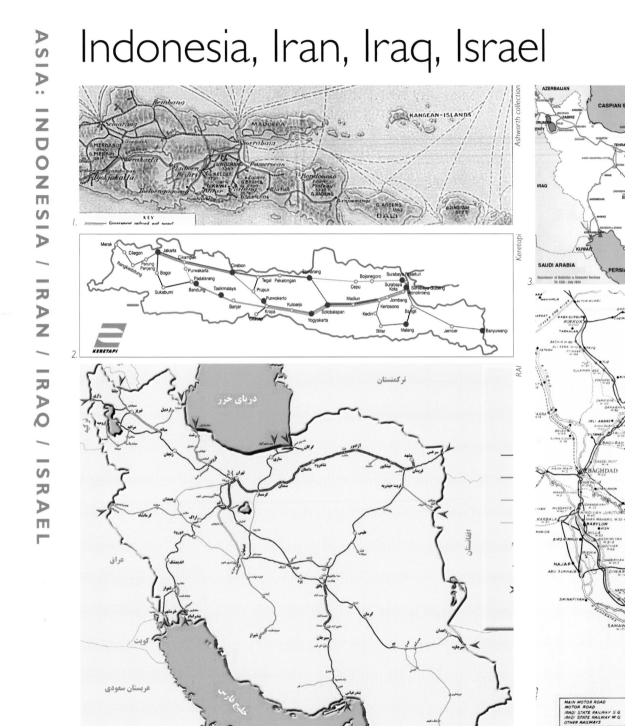

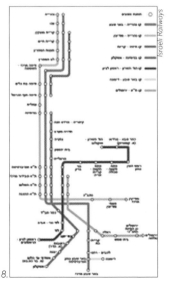

1.

2.

3.

4.

5.

6.

7.

8.

Ashworth collection

Keretapi

RAI

UIC collection

Iraqi Railways

Roger Bragger collection

Palestine Railways

Israeli Railways

ASIA: INDONESIA / IRAN / IRAQ / ISRAEL

106

9.

Japan

9: Chugoku-Shikoku in the 1950s.
10: 1936 map of all Japanese services.
11: 2007 map with numbered stations.
12: Contemporary all Japan schematic.

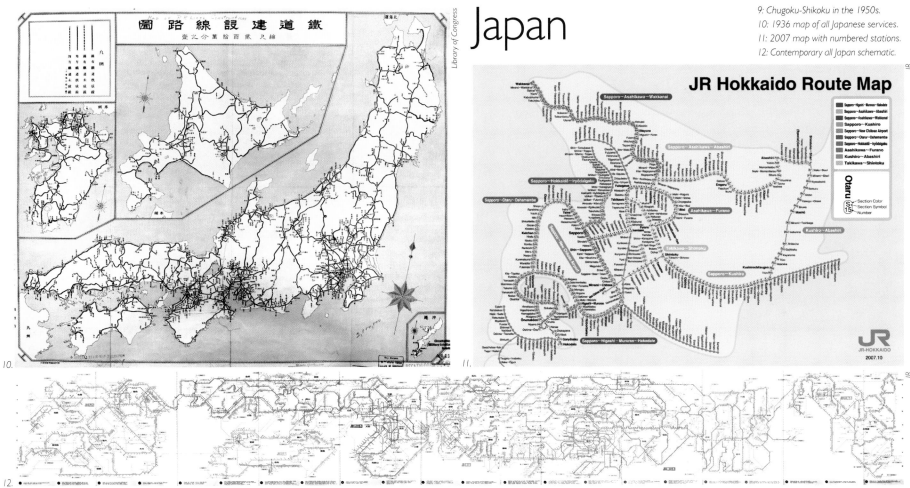

鐵道建設線路圖

縮尺百萬分之壹

10.

11.

12.

JR Hokkaido Route Map

1.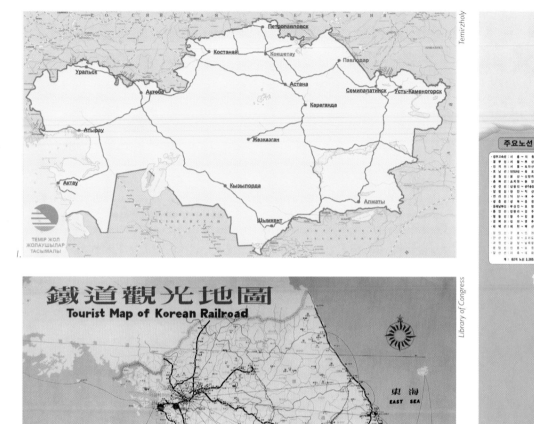

Temirzholy

2.

Library of Congress

鐵道觀光地圖
Tourist Map of Korean Railroad

黃海
YELLOW SEA

東海
EAST SEA

3.

한국철도노선도

2010. 1. 15 현재

범례

주요노선

Korail

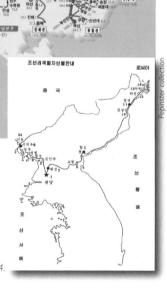

조선려객렬차선별안내

Peprister collection

4.

Kazakhstan,
North Korea,
South Korea

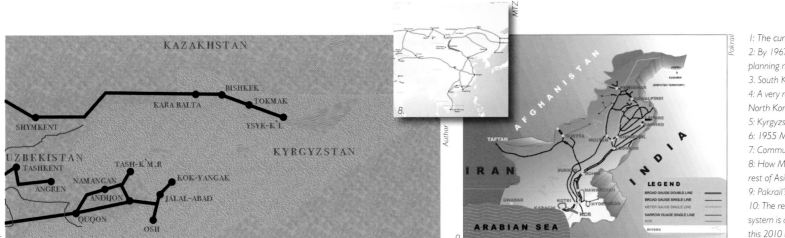

1: The current Kazakhstan network.

2: By 1967 South Korea was already planning major expansion.

3. South Korea's network by 2010.

4: A very rare rail map of the mainline in North Korea from the mid-2000s.

5: Kyrgyzstan unofficial 2010 rail map.

6: 1955 Malayan rail network.

7: Commuter lines into Kuala Lumpur.

8: How Mongolian railways link to the rest of Asia.

9: Pakrail's 2010 network map.

10: The recently refurbished Philippines system is all on Luzon island as seen on this 2010 map.

Kyrgyzstan, Malaysia, Mongolia, Pakistan, Philippines

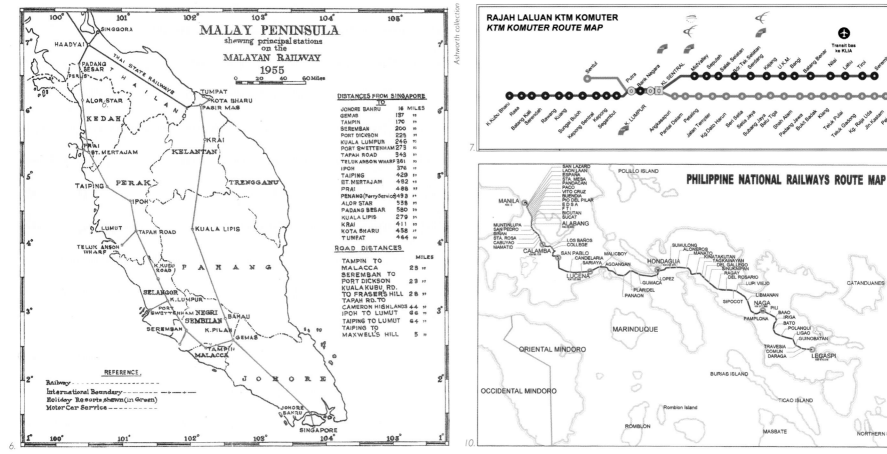

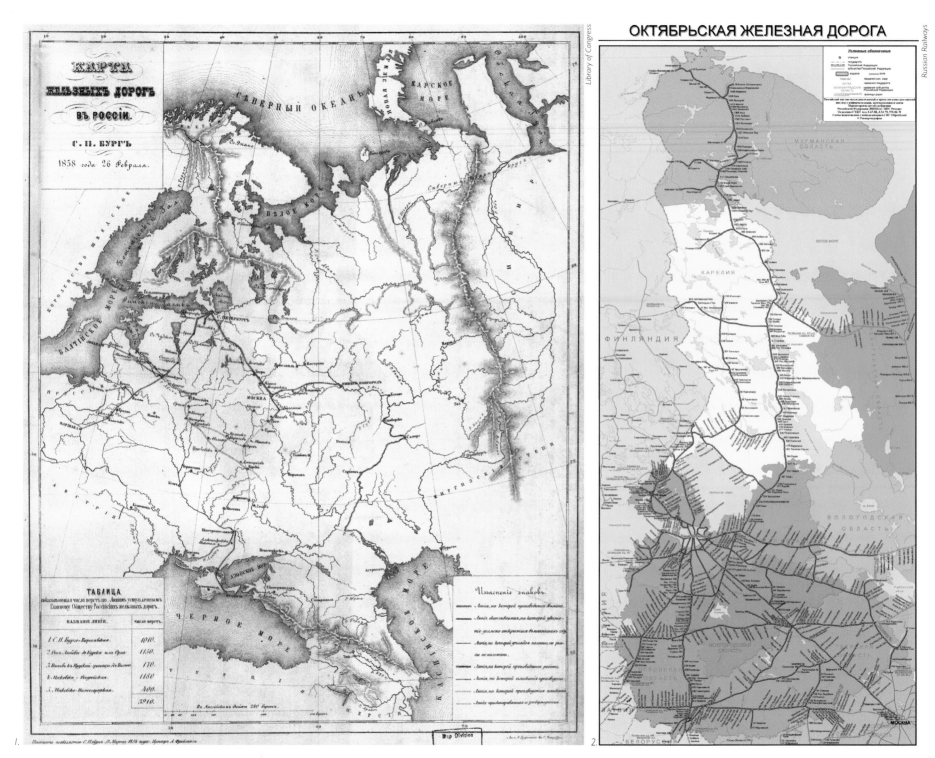

ОКТЯБРЬСКАЯ ЖЕЛЕЗНАЯ ДОРОГА

1.

2.

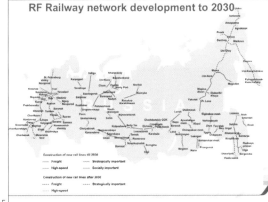

RF Railway network development to 2030

1: 1858 map of the 630 km Moscow–Saint Petersburg line. At this date more train lines emanated from Saint Petersburg than Moscow.

2: 2010 Russian Railways map of the lines radiating from Saint Petersburg.

3: By 1911 many privately financed lines had been built across the vast country, linking hundreds of previously isolated settlements.

4: 2010 map of Russian Railways services along the central and eastern corridor routes.

5: Russian Railways' latest proposals for upgrades and high-speed plans by 2030.

The Russian Federation

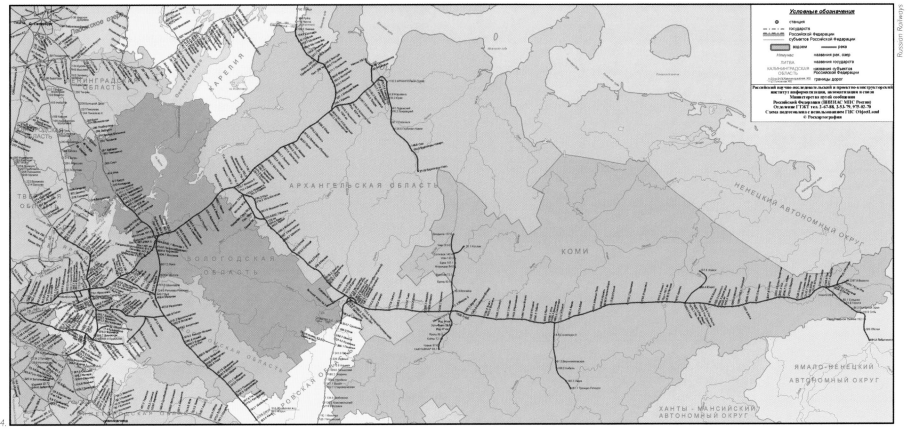

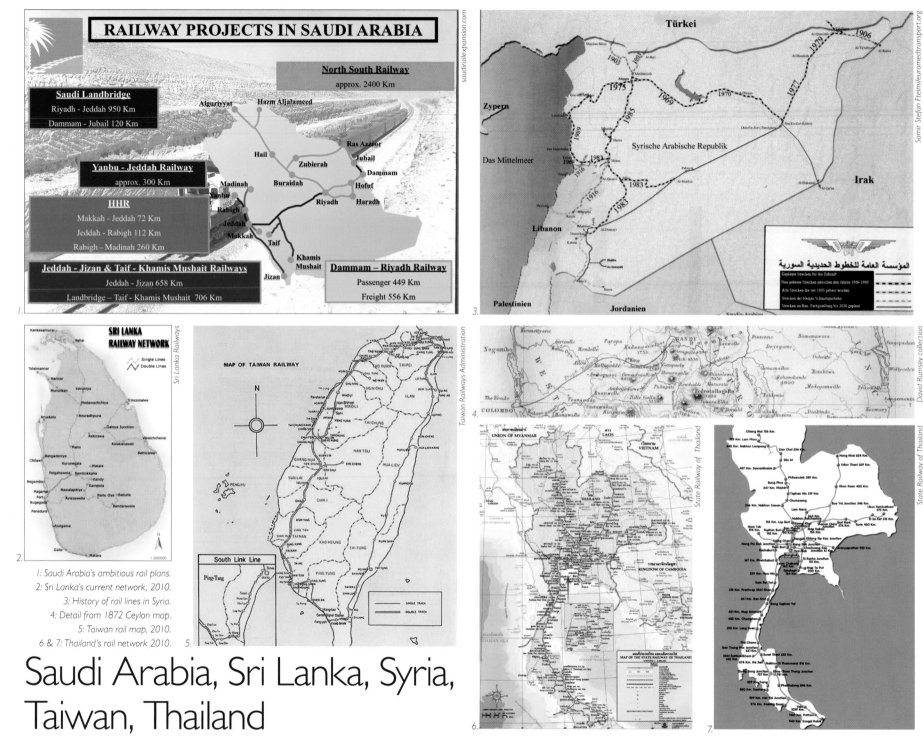

RAILWAY PROJECTS IN SAUDI ARABIA

North South Railway
approx. 2400 Km

Saudi Landbridge
Riyadh - Jeddah 950 Km
Dammam - Jubail 120 Km

Yanbu - Jeddah Railway
approx. 300 Km

HHR
Makkah - Jeddah 72 Km
Jeddah - Rabigh 112 Km
Rabigh - Madinah 260 Km

Jeddah - Jizan & Taif - Khamis Mushait Railways
Jeddah - Jizan 658 Km
Landbridge – Taif - Khamis Mushait 706 Km

Dammam – Riyadh Railway
Passenger 449 Km
Freight 556 Km

saudirailexpansion.com

Samir Stefan Freimileuromedtransport.org

Türkei
Zypern
Das Mittelmeer
Syrische Arabische Republik
Irak
Libanon
Palestinien
Jordanien

المؤسسة العامة للخطوط الحديدية السورية

SRI LANKA RAILWAY NETWORK

Single Lines
Double Lines

Sri Lanka Railways

MAP OF TAIWAN RAILWAY

N

South Link Line

SINGLE TRACK
DOUBLE TRACK

Taiwan Railways Administration

David Rumsey collection

UNION OF MYANMAR

LAOS

VIETNAM

THAILAND

KINGDOM OF CAMBODIA

MAP OF THE STATE RAILWAY OF THAILAND

State Railway of Thailand

State Railway of Thailand

1: Saudi Arabia's ambitious rail plans.
2: Sri Lanka's current network, 2010.
3: History of rail lines in Syria.
4: Detail from 1872 Ceylon map.
5: Taiwan rail map, 2010.
6 & 7: Thailand's rail network 2010.

Saudi Arabia, Sri Lanka, Syria, Taiwan, Thailand

9.

TCDD DEMİRYOLU ŞEBEKESİ

KARADENIZ

1. BÖLGE

2. BÖLGE
ANKARA

7. BÖLGE
AFYON

3. BÖLGE

4. BÖLGE
SIVAS

5. BÖLGE
MALATYA

6. BÖLGE
ADANA

EGE DENIZI

AKDENIZ

10.

KAZAKHSTAN

UZBEKISTAN

TURKMENISTAN

IRAN

AFGHANISTAN

11.

Turkey, Turkmenistan, Uzbekistan, Vietnam

8: Unofficial diagram of the potential future rail network in Thailand.

9: There have been many proposals for new lines in Turkey, including those shown in this detail from a 1941 French map, but most were not constructed.

10: The 2010 Turkish rail network.

11: Unofficial Turkmenistan map.

12: 2010 Russian map of Uzbekistan rail network (in black).

13: Recent map of the Vietnam rail network.

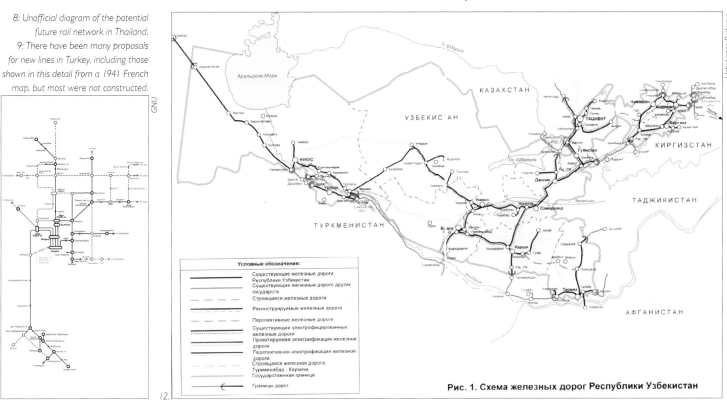

Рис. 1. Схема железных дорог Республики Узбекистан

Условные обозначения:

8.

12.

13.

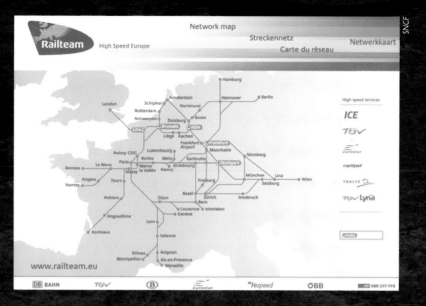

FACING PAGE: A French 1920s children's board game based on actual rail routes radiating from Paris.

E U R O P E

CENTER: All of Europe's main centers connected by the Railteam high speed network, 2009.

The crisscrossed continent

HSH

nicospilt.com

SNCB

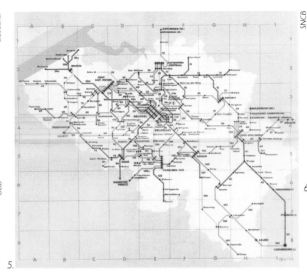

OBB

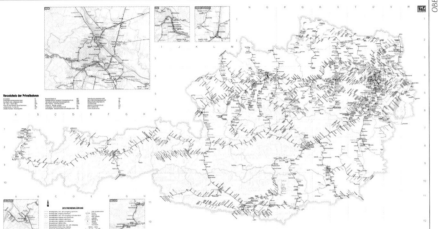

http://szliachta.org

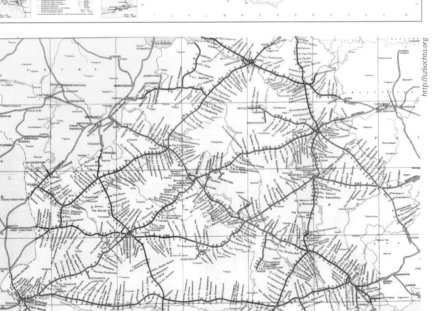

Albania, Austria, Belarus, Belgium

Baedeker

1: What's left of the Albanian network on a 2009 diagram.
2: Detail from Baedeker's 1899 rail map of the Austrian Empire.
3: OBB's current services in Austria, summer 2010.
4: The large Belarus rail system on a current 2010 plan.
5: 1995 version of the Belgian network on a card folder.
6: 1960s diagram of key intercity connecting services in the Benelux.
7: Current bilingual version of the SNCB passenger network, 2010.

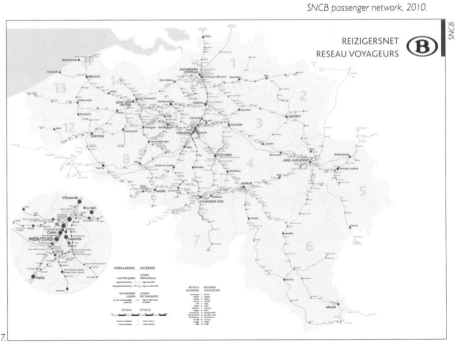

SNCB

Bosnia & Herzegovina, Bulgaria, Croatia, Czech Republic

8: 2010 ZRS services in the Republika Srpska of Bosnia and Herzegovina.
9: ZFBH services in the Federation of Bosnia and Herzegovina.
10: Croatia's rail services in 2010.
11: 2010 Bulgaria train tracks.
12: The Czech Republic, 2010.

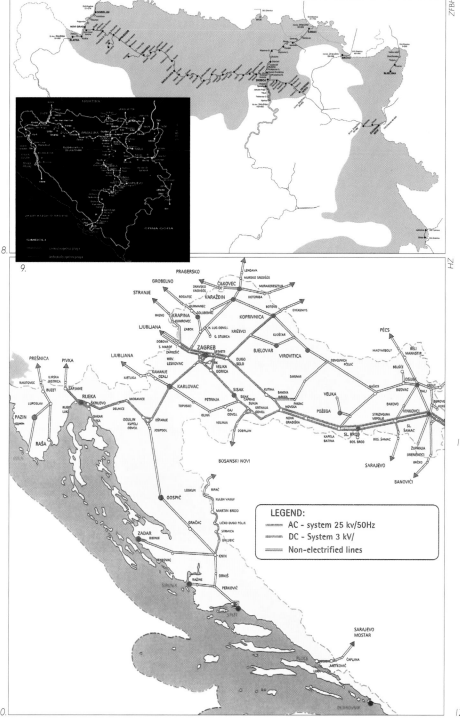

8.

9.

LEGEND:
AC – system 25 kv/50Hz
DC – System 3 kV/
Non-electrified lines

10.

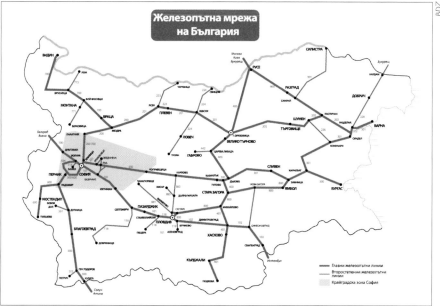

Железопътна мрежа на България

Главни железопътни линии
Второстепенни железопътни линии
Крайградска зона София

11.

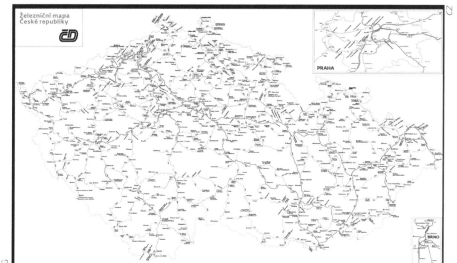

Železniční mapa České republiky

PRAHA

BRNO

12.

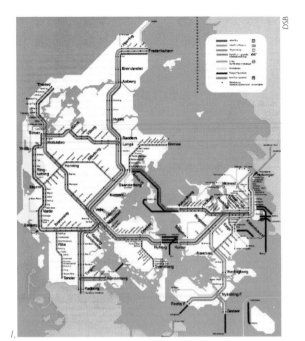

1.

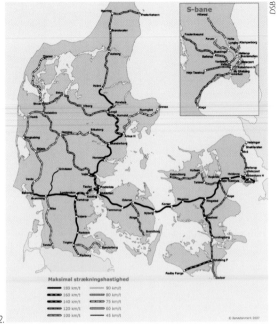

2.

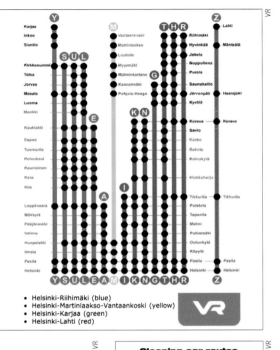

6.

- Helsinki-Riihimäki (blue)
- Helsinki-Martinlaakso-Vantaankoski (yellow)
- Helsinki-Karjaa (green)
- Helsinki-Lahti (red)

Denmark, Estonia, Finland

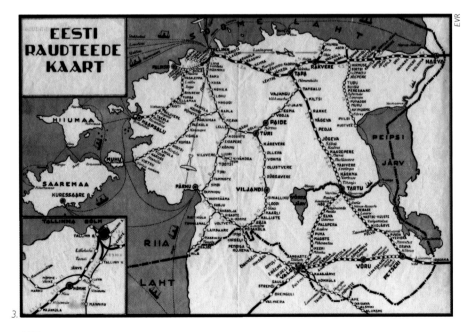

3.

4.

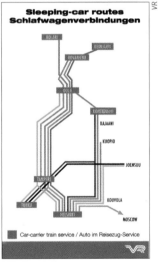

5.

1: 1990s schematic of Danish railroads.
2: Current 2010 Danish network.
3: Official map of Estonia's system.
4: The key cities served by rail connections in Finland.
5: Long-distance sleeper services from Helsinki on a stylish VR 2002 diagram.
6: Unusual linear schematic of the Helsinki suburban rail system, 2010.

France

7: Detail from an 1856 PLM map of
lines heading south from Paris.
8: 1915 map of Corsica from a French
PLM company tourist guidebook.
9: Detail from a vast hand-painted
1920s mural map in the booking hall at
Bordeaux's Gare Saint-Jean.
10: The 2010 French SNCF network
with high-speed TGV lines in blue. 10.

LE RESEAU VOYAGEURS

Ligne à grande vitesse
Ligne à grande vitesse en construction
Ligne classique

SNCF

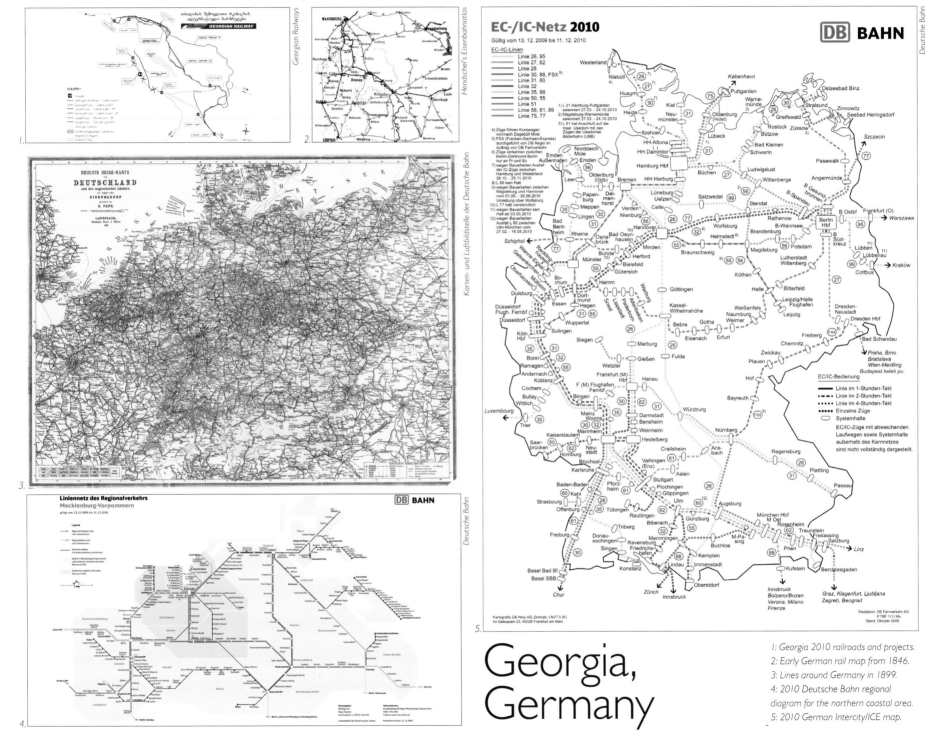

Georgian Railways

Hendschel's Eisenbahnatlas

Karten- und Luftbildstelle der Deutsche Bahn

Deutsche Bahn

Deutsche Bahn

Georgia, Germany

1: Georgia 2010 railroads and projects.

2: Early German rail map from 1846.

3: Lines around Germany in 1899.

4: 2010 Deutsche Bahn regional diagram for the northern coastal area.

5: 2010 German Intercity/ICE map.

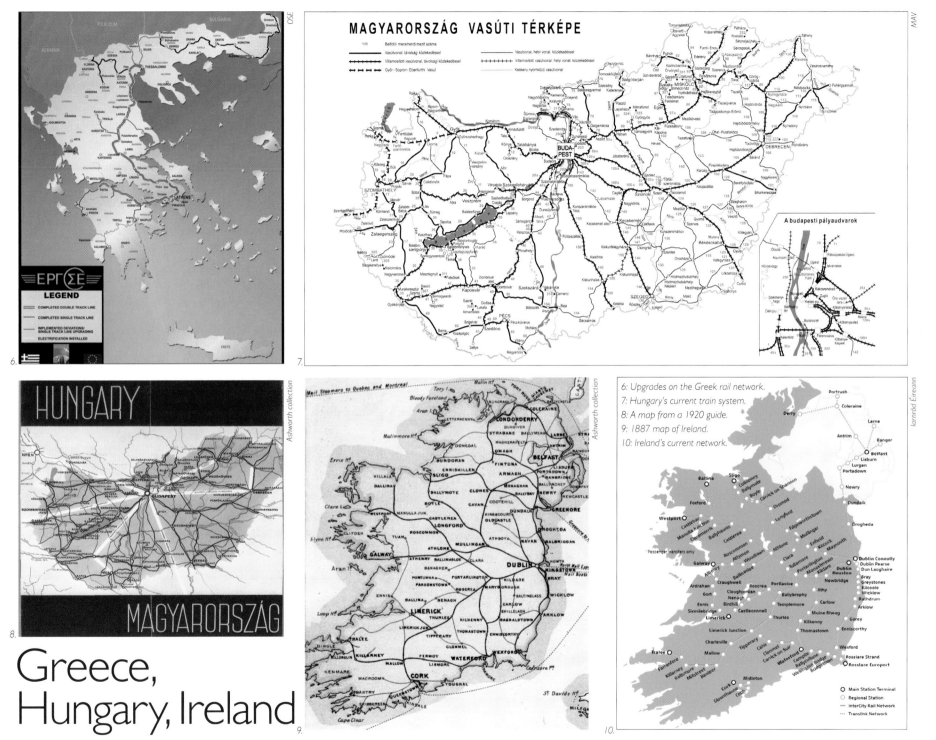

MAGYARORSZÁG VASÚTI TÉRKÉPE

A budapesti pályaudvarok

HUNGARY

MAGYARORSZÁG

6: Upgrades on the Greek rail network.
7: Hungary's current train system.
8: A map from a 1920 guide.
9: 1887 map of Ireland.
10: Ireland's current network.

Greece,
Hungary, Ireland

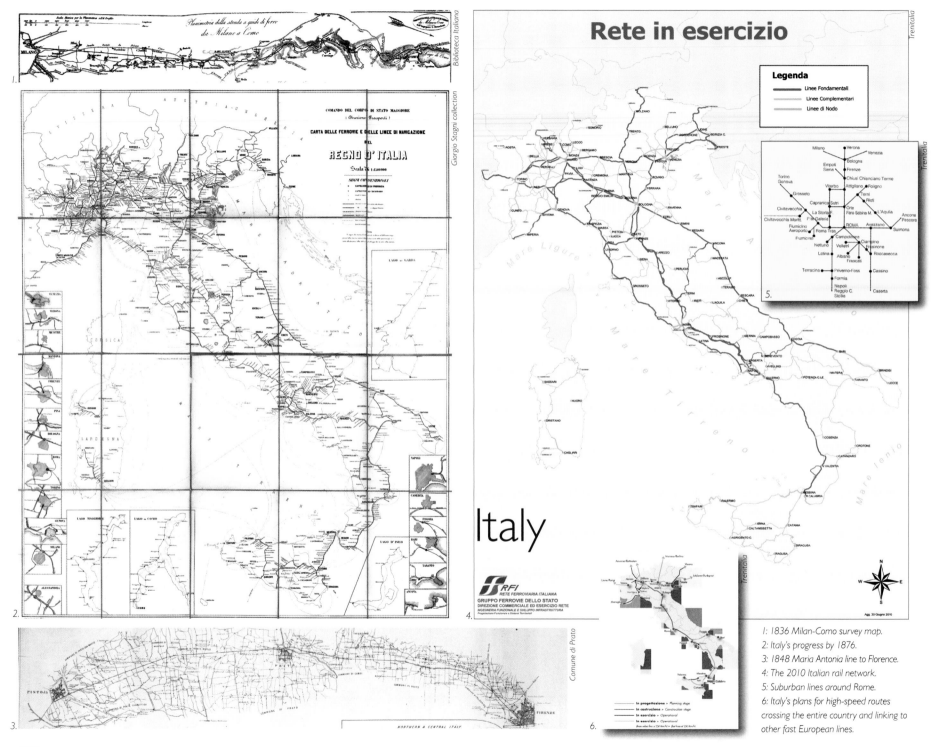

Rete in esercizio

Legenda
- Linee Fondamentali
- Linee Complementari
- Linee di Nodo

COMANDO DEL CORPO DI STATO MAGGIORE
(Direzione Trasporti)

CARTA DELLE FERROVIE E DELLE LINEE DI NAVIGAZIONE
DEL

REGNO D'ITALIA

Scala di 1:1500000

SEGNI CONVENZIONALI

Italy

RFI
RETE FERROVIARIA ITALIANA
GRUPPO FERROVIE DELLO STATO
DIREZIONE COMMERCIALE ED ESERCIZIO RETE
INGEGNERIA FUNZIONALE E SVILUPPO INFRASTRUTTURA

1: 1836 Milan-Como survey map.
2: Italy's progress by 1876.
3: 1848 Maria Antonia line to Florence.
4: The 2010 Italian rail network.
5: Suburban lines around Rome.
6: Italy's plans for high-speed routes crossing the entire country and linking to other fast European lines.

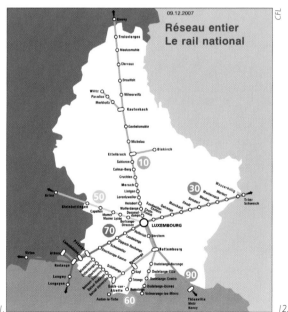

7: Kosovo's rail lines, 2010.
8: Latvia's rail services in 2008.
9: Latvia's rail network in 2010.
10: Lithuanian plans for 2012.
11: Luxembourg's rail network, 2007.
12: Rail routes in Macedonia, 2010.
13: Unofficial Moldova map, 2005.
14: Montenegro on 2006 UN map.

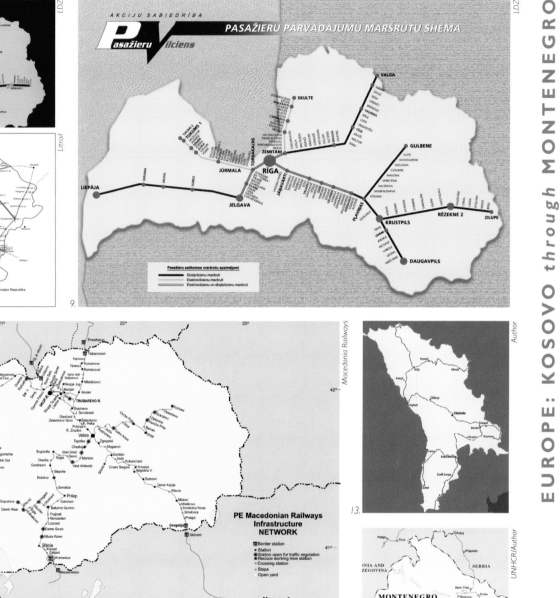

Kosovo, Latvia, Lithuania, Luxembourg, Macedonia, Moldova, Montenegro

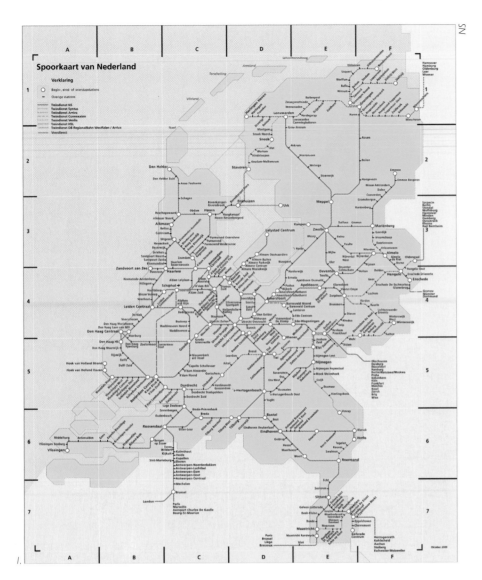

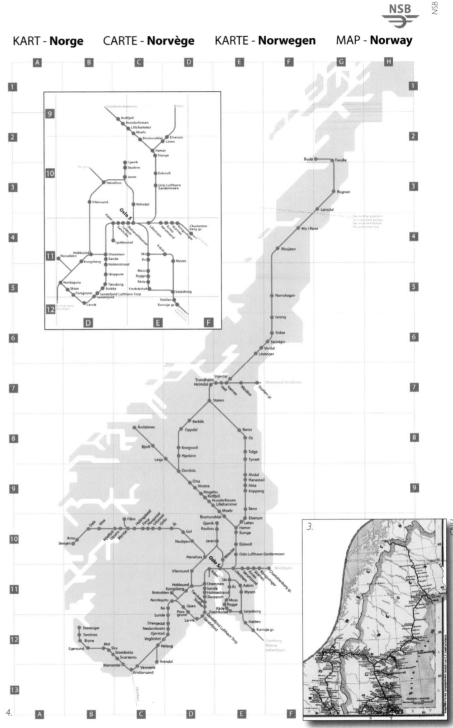

Netherlands, Norway

1: 2010 Netherlands—the system has
used schematics since the 1970s. The
yellow background matches their livery.
2: Dutch simplification on 1895 map.
3: 1897 map of routes from Oslo.
4: National Norwegian rail network
provided by NSB, 2010.

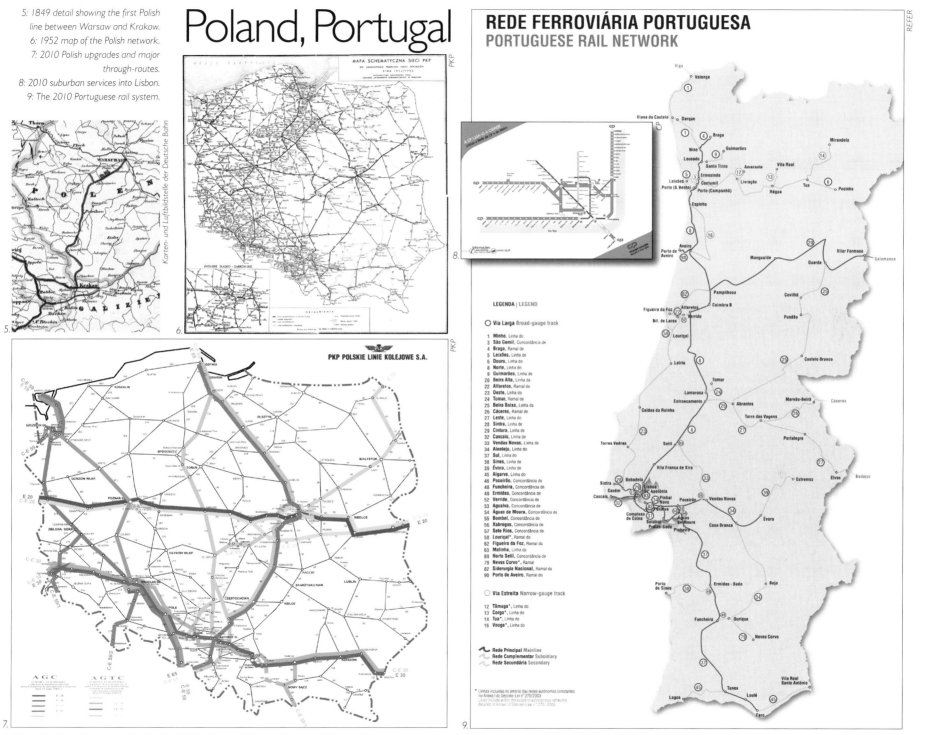

5: 1849 detail showing the first Polish line between Warsaw and Krakow.
6: 1952 map of the Polish network.
7: 2010 Polish upgrades and major through-routes.
8: 2010 suburban services into Lisbon.
9: The 2010 Portuguese rail system.

Poland, Portugal

Karten- und Luftbildstelle der Deutsche Bahn

MAPA SCHEMATYCZNA SIECI PKP

PKP

PKP POLSKIE LINIE KOLEJOWE S.A.

PKP

REDE FERROVIÁRIA PORTUGUESA
PORTUGUESE RAIL NETWORK

LEGENDA | LEGEND

○ **Via Larga** Broad-gauge track

1 **Minho**, Linha do
3 **São Gemil**, Concordância de
4 **Braga**, Ramal de
5 **Leixões**, Linha de
6 **Douro**, Linha do
8 **Norte**, Linha do
9 **Guimarães**, Linha de
20 **Beira Alta**, Linha da
22 **Alfarelos**, Ramal de
23 **Oeste**, Linha do
24 **Tomar**, Ramal de
25 **Beira Baixa**, Linha da
26 **Cáceres**, Ramal de
27 **Leste**, Linha do
28 **Sintra**, Linha de
29 **Cintura**, Linha de
32 **Cascais**, Linha do
33 **Vendas Novas**, Linha de
34 **Alentejo**, Linha do
37 **Sul**, Linha do
38 **Sines**, Linha de
39 **Évora**, Linha de
45 **Algarve**, Linha do
46 **Poceirão**, Concordância de
48 **Funcheira**, Concordância de
52 **Ermidas**, Concordância de
52 **Verride**, Concordância de
53 **Agualva**, Concordância de
54 **Águas de Moura**, Concordância de
55 **Bombel**, Concordância de
56 **Xabregas**, Concordância de
57 **Sete Rios**, Concordância de
58 **Louriçal***, Ramal do
62 **Figueira da Foz**, Ramal da
63 **Matinha**, Linha do
69 **Norte Setil**, Concordância de
79 **Neves Corvo***, Ramal
82 **Siderurgia Nacional**, Ramal da
90 **Porto de Aveiro**, Ramal do

○ **Via Estreita** Narrow-gauge track

12 **Tâmega***, Linha do
13 **Corgo***, Linha do
14 **Tua***, Linha do
16 **Vouga***, Linha do

〰 **Rede Principal** Mainline
〰 **Rede Complementar** Subsidiary
〰 **Rede Secundária** Secondary

* Linhas incluídas no âmbito das redes autónomas constantes no Anexo I do Decreto-Lei nº 270/2003
Lines include within the scope of autonomous networks detailed in Annex I of Decree-Law nº 270/2003

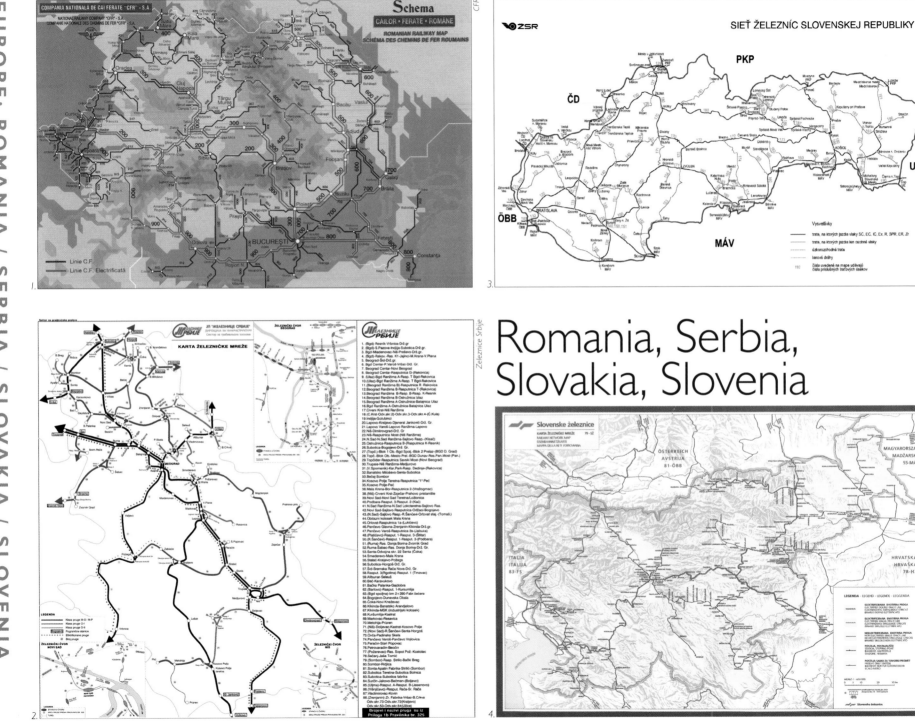

Romania, Serbia, Slovakia, Slovenia

ADIF

GNU

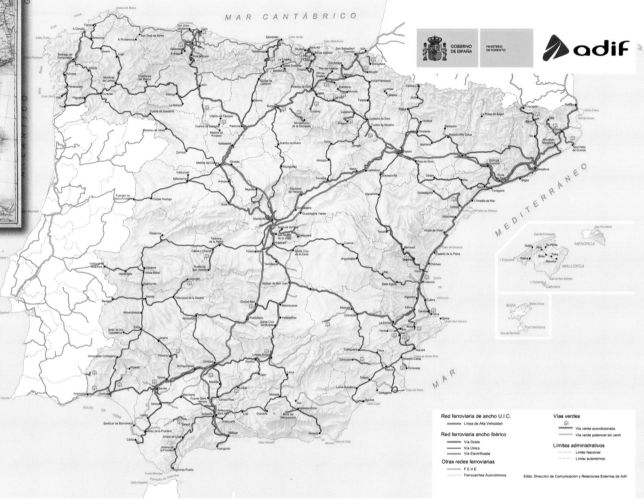

Spain

1: 2010 Romanian train network.
2: Rail services in Serbia, 2010.
3: The 2010 Slovak rail network.
4: 2010 Slovenia Rail geographic map.
5: The Iberian Peninsula in 1864.
6: Though Spain had yet to emerge as a tourist destination, a 1958 RENFE diagram exhibits some stylish aspects.
7: 1974 RENFE station wall map.
8: 2009 map of top speeds possible on the various main lines produced by rail infrastructure agency ADIF.
9: All current lines in Spain—note that ADIF and other agencies have converted many old rail alignments into green linear parks and walkways.

9.

Red ferroviaria de ancho U.I.C.
Línea de Alta Velocidad

Vías verdes
Vía verde acondicionada
Vía verde potencial sin carril

Red ferroviaria ancho Ibérico
Vía Doble
Vía Única
Vía Electrificada

Límites administrativos
Límite Nacional
Límite autonómico

Otras redes ferroviarias
F.E.V.E.
Ferrocarriles Autonómicos

Edita: Dirección de Comunicación y Relaciones Externas de Adif.

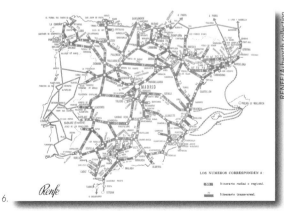

6.

RENFE/Ashworth collection

7.

RENFE/Ashworth collection

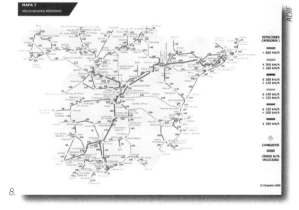

8.

ADIF

Railway map of the nordic countries

Geltungsbereich Generalabonnement
Rayon de validité abonnement général
Raggio di validità abbonamento generale

SBB CFF FFS

Verkehrsmittel
Moyens de transport
Mezzi di trasporto

Sweden,
Switzerland,
Ukraine

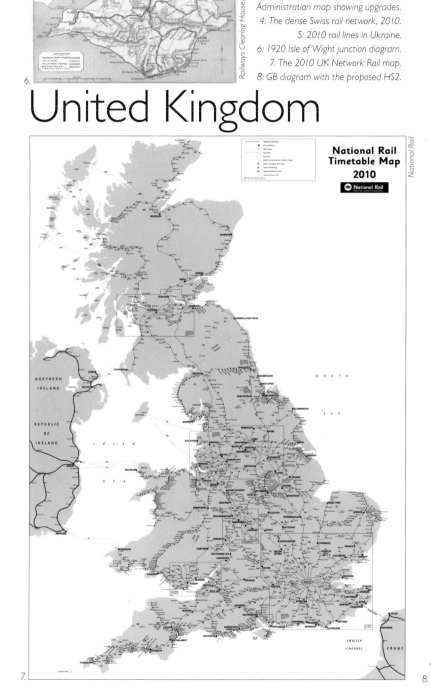

United Kingdom

1: Sweden 2010 in Scandinavia's heart.
2: Southern Sweden in 1910.
3: 2010 Swedish Transport
Administration map showing upgrades.
4: The dense Swiss rail network, 2010.
5: 2010 rail lines in Ukraine.
6: 1920 Isle of Wight junction diagram.
7: The 2010 UK Network Rail map.
8: GB diagram with the proposed HS2.

Railways Clearing House/GNU/BRBR

6.

National Rail Timetable Map 2010

National Rail

7.

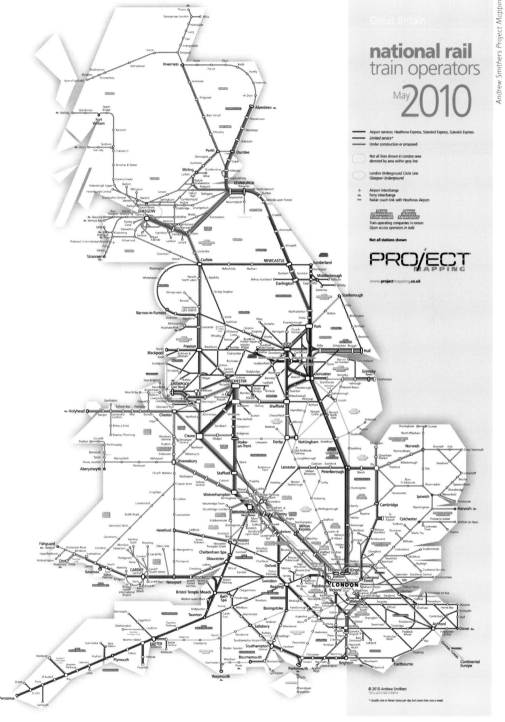

Andrew Smithers: Project Mapping

Great Britain

national rail train operators May 2010

8.

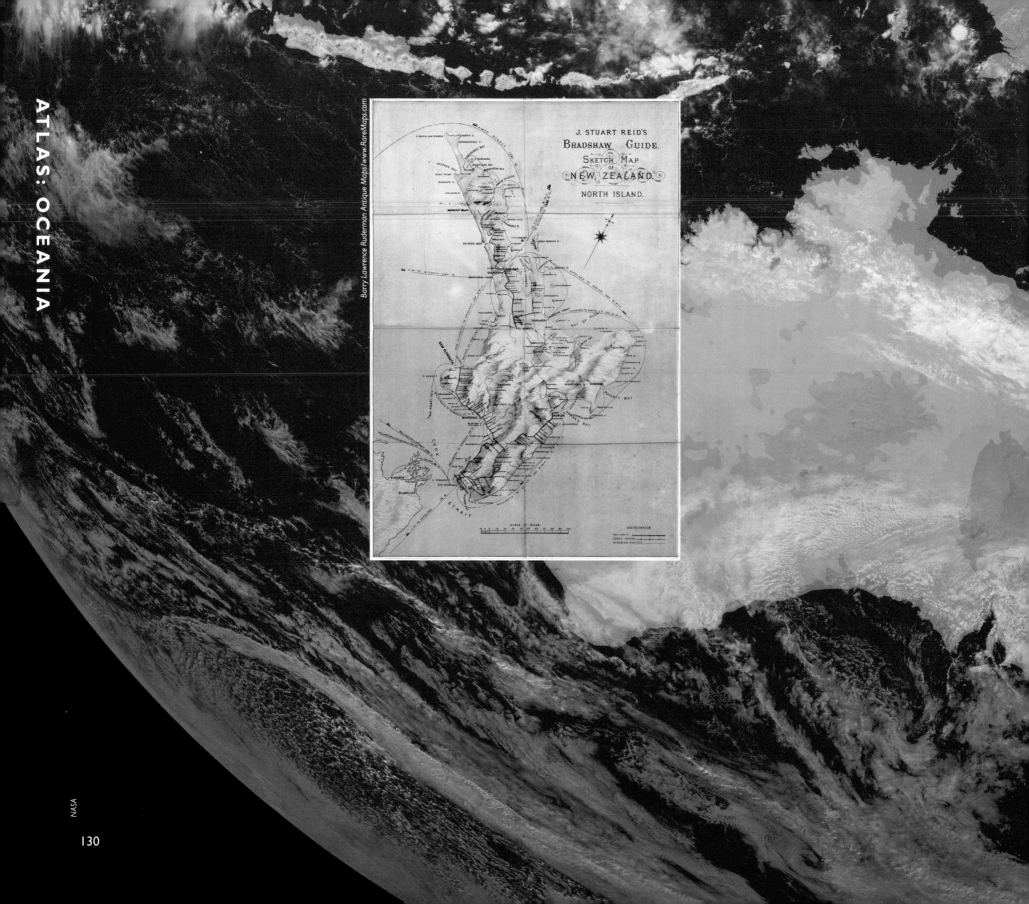

J. STUART REID'S
Bradshaw Guide.
Sketch Map
OF
NEW ZEALAND.
NORTH ISLAND.

OCEANIA
Just two rail networks survive

TOP: Though radical thinkers had big plans for railroad building in Australia, like Alex Wilson's 1909 idea for a line to Darwin, few grand schemes were realized—the far northern region was only reached in 2004.
FACING: A good start was made in New Zealand, as this late 1800s Bradshaw's map shows, but over a thousand kilometers was closed in the mid-twentieth century.

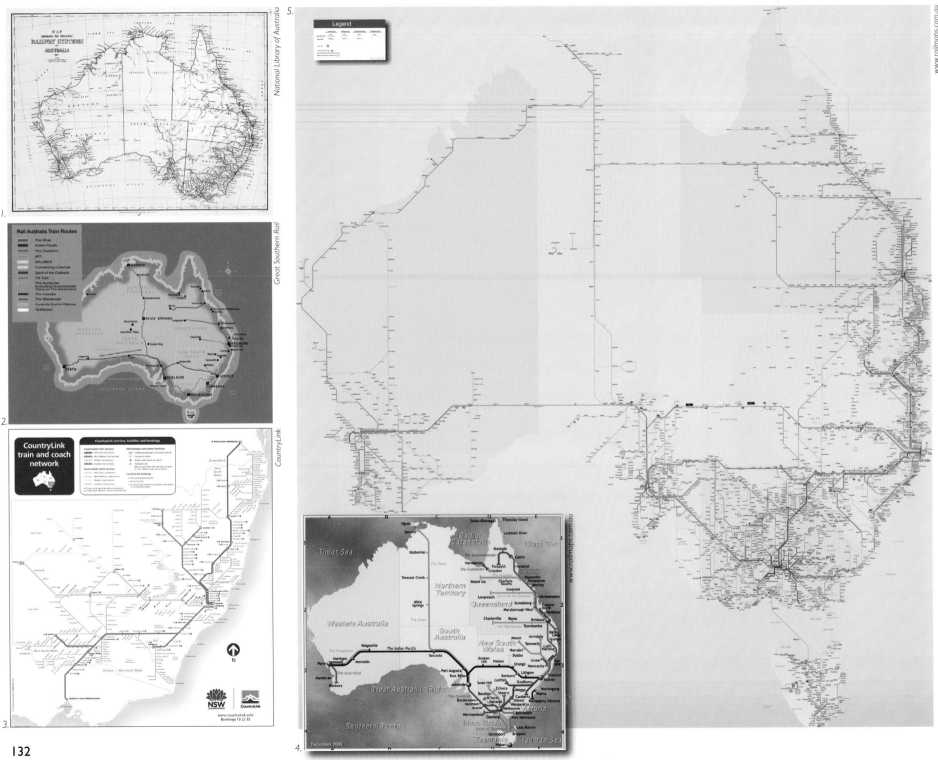

1.

Rail Australia Train Routes

2.

CountryLink
train and coach
network

www.countrylink.info
Bookings 13 22 32

3.

4. December 2009

5.

Legend

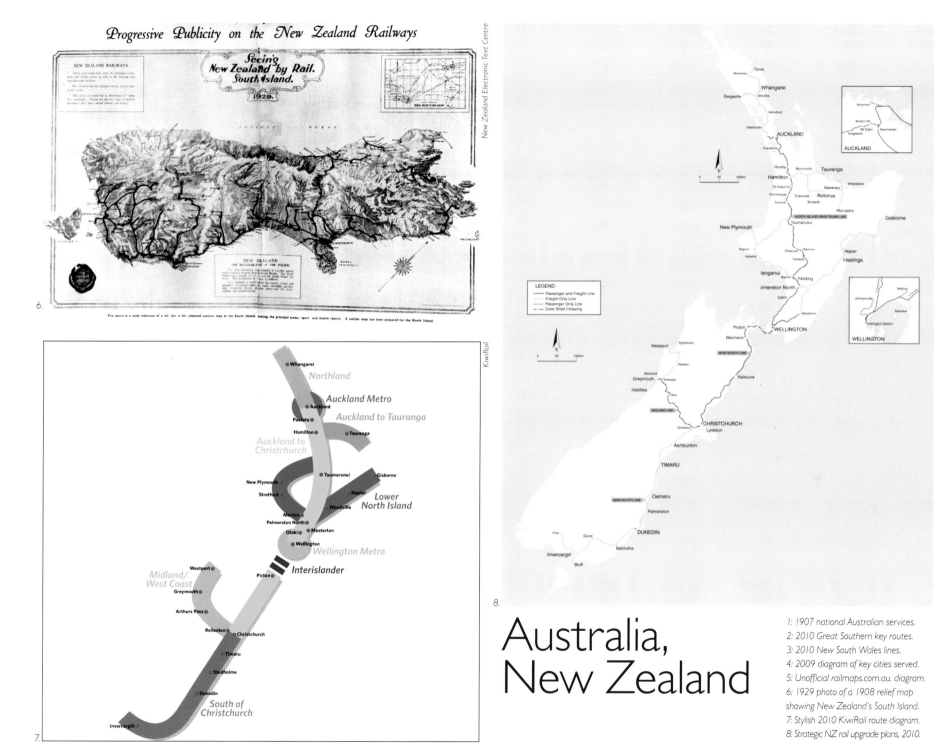

New Zealand Electronic Text Centre

KiwiRail

Ministry of Transport, New Zealand

6.

7.

8.

Australia,
New Zealand

1: 1907 national Australian services.

2: 2010 Great Southern key routes.

3: 2010 New South Wales lines.

4: 2009 diagram of key cities served.

5: Unofficial railmaps.com.au. diagram.

6: 1929 photo of a 1908 relief map
showing New Zealand's South Island.

7: Stylish 2010 KiwiRail route diagram.

8: Strategic NZ rail upgrade plans, 2010.

T R A C K S T A T S

COUNTRY/TERRITORY (ENGLISH NAME)	TRACK LENGTH IN KILOMETERS PEAK (YEAR)	NOW	PLANNED	OPERATOR WEB SITE (all www. unless stated)
WORLD	2,500,000 (1920)	1,370,782	300,000	uic.org
AFRICA				
ALGERIA	5,014 (1946)	3,572	2,630HS	sntf.dz
ANGOLA	2,995 (1977)	194	1,000	cpires.com/benguela
BENIN	758 (Cl: 2007?)	578		OCBN
BOTSWANA	888 (Internal passenger service closed: 2009)			botswanarailways.co.bw
BURKINA FASO		622		mith.gov.bf
CAMEROON	1,173 (1976)	974		camrail.net
CONGO (DEM REP)	5,138 (1995)	3,641		ic-lubum.cd/sncc
CONGO (REP OF THE)	886	795		cfco.cg OR onatra.info
DJIBOUTI	781	100		train-franco-ethiopien.com
EGYPT	5.063 (2005)	5,063	>200	egyptrail.gov.eg
ERITREA	337	118		Eritrean Railway/eritrea.be/railway
ETHIOPIA	1,088 (1977)	681	>5,000	train-franco-ethiopien.com
GABON	810	670	250	Trans-Gabon Railway (SETRAG/OCTRA)/Transgabonais
GHANA	953 (1976)	935	500	Ghana Railway Corporation
GUINEA	1,086	837	1,000	guinee.gov.gn
IVORY COAST	1,173 (1976)	639	170	SITARAIL/Comazar
KENYA	5,893 (1976)	2,778		Kenya Railways Corporation/riftvalleyrailways.com
LESOTHO		3		Administered by South African Railways
LIBERIA	490 (Cl: 2003)	0	260	mot.gov.lr
LIBYA	400 (Cl: 1965)	0	3,170	railroads.org.ly
MADAGASCAR	884 (1976)	673		madarail.mg
MALAWI	797 (2001)	615		Central East African Railways/yellowtrains.com
MALI	733	729		Chemin de fer du Dakar-Niger
MAURITANIA	728	704 (f)		snim.com/fr/train
MAURITIUS	250 (Cl: 1964)	0	25	gov.mu
MOROCCO	2,071 (1976)	1,989	170/600HS	oncf.ma
MOZAMBIQUE	3,696 (1976)	3,116	>400	cfmnet.co.mz
NAMIBIA		2,382	47	transnamib.com.na
NIGERIA	3,886 (2003)	3,505	277	nrc-ng.org
RWANDA	0	0	>200	mininfra.gov.rw
SENEGAL	1,034	906	750	Chemin de fer du Dakar-Niger
SIERRA LEONE	84 (Cl: 1974)	0		Sierra Leone Government Railway
SOUTH AFRICA	24,487 (1970s)	20,872	80/720HS	shosholozameyl.co.za / prasa.com OR gautrain.co.za
SUDAN	6,424	4,578	>900	sudanrailways.gov.sd
SWAZILAND		301 (f)		SwaziRail
TANZANIA	3,689	2,722		trctz.com OR tazara.co.tz
TOGO	568 (2008)	525	100	republicoftogo.com
TUNISIA	2,257 (1976)	2,145	150	sncft.com.tn
UGANDA	1,244	198		Ugandan Railway Corporation
WESTERN SAHARA		5 (f)		Société Nationale Industrielle et Minière
ZAMBIA	2,157	1,273		Zambia Railways Ltd and tazarasite.com
ZIMBABWE	3,077	2,583		nrz.co.zw
AMERICA NORTH				
CANADA	92,449 (1976)	49,422	>2,000HS	cn.ca OR cpr.ca OR viarail.ca
COSTA RICA	440 (Cl: 1995)	15		INCOFER casapres.go.cr
CUBA	8,598	5,076		Ferrocarriles de Cuba/cubagob.cu
DOMINICAN REPUBLIC	1,784	1,139 (f)		centralromana.com
GUATEMALA	885	332 (Cl: 1995–2007)		ferroviasgt.com
HONDURAS	786 (1993)	699		Ferrocarril Nacional de Honduras
JAMAICA	330 (Cl: 1992)	0		mtw.gov.jm/dep_agencies/ja_rail
MEXICO	17,516	27	215	fsuburbanos.com
NICARAGUA	382	6 (Cl: 2001)		mti.gob.nr
PANAMA		76		panarail.com
PUERTO RICO	96	25		ati.gobierno.pr
SALVADOR, EL	602 (1976)	283 (Cl: 2002)		fenadesal.gob.sv
ST. KITTS & NEVIS	50	29		stkittsscenicrailway.com
TRINIDAD & TOBAGO	173 (Cl: 1968)	0	98	trinitrain.co.tt
UNITED STATES	408,777 (1918)	226,427	3,000	amtrak.com
AMERICA SOUTH				
ARGENTINA	47,000 (1948)	34,059	710HS	cnrt.gov.ar OR argentina.gov.ar
BOLIVIA	3,627 (1974)	2,866		supertransporte.gov.co/super OR fcab.cl
BRAZIL	29,817	27,882	518HS	rffsa.gov.br OR transportes.gov.br
CHILE	5,898	5,481		efe.cl
COLOMBIA	3,802	2,761	177	ferrovias.gov.co
ECUADOR	965 (Cl: 1998)	0	>100	efe.gov.ec
GUYANA	127	127 (f)		gina.gov.gy/ministries
PARAGUAY	441 (1976)	36 (Cl: 2006)		ferrocarriles.com.py
PERU	4,500	2,528	722	perurail.com
SURINAME	166	166?		mintct.sr
URUGUAY	2,993	1,641		afe.com.uy
VENEZUELA	806	682	963	ife.gob.ve

COUNTRY/TERRITORY	PEAK (YEAR)	NOW	PLANNED	OPERATOR WEB SITE
ASIA				
AFGHANISTAN	25	47	14,000	ands.gov.af
ARMENIA		845		ukzhd.am
AZERBAIJAN	2,932	2,117	98	mintrans.az
BANGLADESH	2,874 (1976)	2,855		railway.gov.bd
BRUNEI		13		jpm-bm.gov.bn
BURMA (MYANMAR)		3,955		mrt.gov.mm
CAMBODIA	649 (1976)	0	612	mpwt.gov.kh
CHINA		86,000	34,000	china-mor.gov.cn
INDIA		64,099	25,000/2,000HS	indianrail.gov.in
INDONESIA	8,529	6,458	130/683HS	kereta-api.co.id
IRAN		8,442	18,900/1,100HS	rai.ir
IRAQ	2,528 (1971)	1,905	>4,000	iraqirailways.com
ISRAEL		949	55HS	rail.co.il
JAPAN		27,268	>450	jr.jp
JORDAN	552 (1974)	251	1,600	arc.gov.jo OR au-railways.org
KAZAKHSTAN		14,205		railways.kz
KOREA (North)		5,235	27	korea-dpr.com
KOREA (South)	5,448	3,391	252HS	korail.com
KYRGYZSTAN	417	320		ktj.kg
LEBANON	401 (Cl: 1997)	0		public-works.gov.lb
MALAYSIA	1,719 (1941)	1,699	320	ktmb.com.my
MONGOLIA	1,425 (1973)	1,810		mtz.mn
NEPAL	102	59	156	nepalgov.gov.np
PAKISTAN	8,808 (1973)	7,791	260HS	railways.gov.pk
PHILIPPINES	1,169 (1972)	479	195HS	pnr.gov.ph
RUSSIAN FEDERATION	145,000 (1945)	86,500	10,887HS	rzd.ru
SAUDI ARABIA		1,018 (f)	1,005	saudirailways.org OR saudirailexpansion.com
SRI LANKA		1,508	127	railway.gov.lk
SYRIA		2,139		cfssyria.org
TAIWAN		1,093	335HS	railway.gov.tw
TAJIKISTAN		680		mintranscom.tj
THAILAND		4,429	2,624	railway.co.th
TURKEY	9,869 (1974)	8,671	5,000/4,000HS	TCDD.gov.tr
TURKMENISTAN	3,181	2,440	722	fahrplancenter.com /TurkmenRailIndex.html
UNITED ARAB EMIRATES		0	>1,000	Union Railways Company of UAE
UZBEKISTAN	4,230	3,950	223	uzrailway.uz/uzb
VIETNAM	1,278 (1976)	3,147	1,560/1,630HS	vr.com.vn
EUROPE				eurail.com OR raileurope.com
ALBANIA	896	>200	>100	mpptt.gov.al
AUSTRIA	5,864 (1976)	5,755	89	oebb.at
BELARUS	5,523	5,491	280	rw.by
BELGIUM	4,811 (1945)	3,374	>50	sncb.be
BOSNIA & HERZEGOVINA	1,103	1,034	70	zfbh.ba
BULGARIA	7,626	4,144	58	bdz.bg
CROATIA		2,974	<100	hznet.hr
CZECH REPUBLIC	13,317 (1976)	9,496	25	cdrail.cz
DENMARK		2,132	300	dsb.dk
ESTONIA	1,013	816	500	evr.ee
FINLAND	5,975	5,865	50	vr.fi
FRANCE	60,000 (1914)	29,213	3712HS	sncf.fr
GEORGIA		1,513	30	railway.ge
GERMANY	43,023 (1977)	41,315	1,100HS	db.de
GREECE	2,551	1,815	520HS	ose.gr
HUNGARY	7,610 (1977)	7,606		mav.hu
IRELAND	5,500 (1920)	1,919	>300	irishrail.ie
ITALY	20,869 (1977)	16,335	710HS	ferroviedellostato.it
KOSOVO		430		kosovorailway.com
LATVIA		2,282	>200	ldz.lv
LITHUANIA		1,766	>350	litrail.lt
LUXEMBOURG	550 (1945)	275		cfl.lu
MACEDONIA (FYR)		699	60	mz.com.mk
MOLDOVA		1,232		railway.md
MONACO		3		sncf.fr
MONTENEGRO		249	12	zcg-prevoz.me
NETHERLANDS		2,809	55/200HS	ns.nl
NORWAY	4,241 (1976)	4,087	40HS	nsb.no
POLAND	23,573 (1977)	19,599	1,500HS	pkp.pl
PORTUGAL	3,592 (1949)	2,603	1,006HS	cp.pt
ROMANIA	11,039 (1976)	10,788	500HS	cfr.ro
SERBIA		3,809	30	serbianrailways.com
SLOVAKIA		3,592	36	zsr.sk
SLOVENIA	>2,730	1,229		slo-zeleznice.si
SPAIN	18,139 (1959)	14,781	9000HS	renfe.es
SWEDEN	11,179 (1976)	9,830	457HS	sj.se
SWITZERLAND	4,478 (1976)	3,619	>50	sbb.ch
UKRAINE		21,676	>2,200HS	uz.gov.ua
UK	31,382 (1907)	16,264	320/>500HS	nationalrail.co.uk OR atoc.org
OCEANIA				
AUSTRALIA	33,096 (1977)	33,819	1,500HS	infrastructure.gov.au/rail
FIJI	644 (1975)	0		transport.gov.fj
NEW ZEALAND	5,721	4,128		kiwirail.co.nz

BIBLIOGRAPHY

A Picture History of the Liverpool-Manchester Railway, Liverpool: Scouse Press, 1970.

Choko, Marc H. & Jones, David L., *Posters of the Canadian Pacific*, Richmond Hill: Firefly Books, 2004.

Clark, John, *Remarkable Maps: 100 Examples of How Cartography Defined, Changed and Stole the World*, London: Conway Maritime Press, 2005.

Cole, Beverley & Durack, Richard, *Railway Posters 1923–1947*, London: Laurence King, 1992.

Cole, Beverley, *Trains: The Early Years*, Königswinter: Könemann/Tandem Verlag/Getty Images, 2001.

———, *Happy as a Sand Boy: Early Railway Posters*, London: HMSO/National Railway Museum, 1990.

Conolly, W. Philip, *British Railways Pre-grouping Atlas and Gazetteer*, London: Ian Allan, 1967.

Dow, Andrew, *Telling the Passenger Where to Get Off*, London: Capital Transport, 2005.

Foxwell, Simon, *Mapping London: Making Sense of the City*, London: Black Dog Publishing, 2007.

Gottwaldt, Alfred, *Das Berliner U- und S-Bahnnetz*, Stuttgart: Transpress Verlag, 2004.

Haresnape, Brian, *British Rail 1948–78: A Journey by Design*, Shepperton: Ian Allan, 1979.

Jacobs, Frank, *Strange Maps: An Atlas of Cartographic Curiosities*, New York: Viking Studio, 2009.

Johnson, Lynn & O'Leary, Michael, *All Aboard: Images from the Golden Age of Rail Travel*, San Francisco: Chronicle Books, 1999.

Nock, O. S., *World Atlas of Railways*, Bristol: Victoria House Publishing, 1983.

Ovenden, Mark, *Transit Maps of the World*, New York: Penguin Books, 2007.

———, *Paris Underground: The Maps, Stations, and Design of the Metro*, New York: Penguin Books, 2009.

Palin, Michael, *Happy Holidays: The Golden Age of Railway Posters*, London: Guild Publishing, 1987.

Railway Directory & Yearbook 1977, London: IPC Transport Press, 1976.

Simmons, Jack & Biddle, Gordon (editors), *The Oxford Companion to British Railway History*, Oxford: Oxford University Press, 2000.

Stover, John, *The Routledge Historical Atlas of the American Railroads*, New York: Routledge, 1999.

Wigg, Julia, *Bon Voyage! Travel Posters of the Edwardian Era*, Norwich: Public Record Office/Her Majesty's Stationery Office, 1996.

Wildbur, Peter & Burke, Michael, *Information Graphics: Innovative Solutions in Contemporary Design*, London: Thames & Hudson, 1998.

Wolmar, Christian, *Fire & Steam: How the Railways Transformed Britain*, London: Atlantic Books, 2007.

———, *Blood, Iron & Gold: How the Railways Transformed the World*, London: Atlantic Books, 2009.

Yenne, Bill, *Atlas of North American Railroads*, St. Paul: MBI Publishing, 2005.

Zeber, Michael & Gruber, John, *Travel by Train: The American Railroad Poster, 1870–1950*, Bloomington: Indiana University Press, 2002.

WEBOGRAPHY

Since this is an international project (and authors of such books are not yet in possession of world rail travel passes—hint, hint!), a large proportion of the research was made online. It is not possible on this page to list all Web resources consulted, but now that most rail operators have Web pages (see "Trackstats" facing page), the latest rail map can usually be found for any given country on those. Although some rail operators' Web designers would be wise to place an unambiguous direct link to their rail network map on the home page as opposed to burying it in a company report or locking it to Google Maps, Flash players, and the like. It is not that hard to commission a national rail map these days and it would certainly be of great benefit to passengers and researchers alike! Having noted those words, here is a list of some of the other sites that the author found most useful in preparing this book. (All addresses preceeded by www. unless stated.)

Australian Rail Maps:
railmaps.com.au

Barry Lawrence Ruderman Antique Maps Inc.:
raremaps.com

Bibliothèque Nationale de France:
http://catalogue.bnf.fr OR http://gallica.bnf.fr

British Library Map Room:
bl.uk/reshelp/bldept/maps/index.html

California State Railway Museum:
csrmf.org

Central Office of Intelligence World Factbook:
cia.gov/library/publications/the-world-factbook/index.html

David Rumsey Collection:
davidrumsey.com

Historical New Jersey Railroad Maps:
mapmaker.rutgers.edu/historicalmaps/railroads/railroads.html

History Map:
history-map.com

International Union of Railways (UIC):
—Members list: uic.org/apps

Joho Maps:
johomaps.com

Library of Congress:
http://memory.loc.gov/ammem/gmdhtml/rrhtml/rrhome.html

The Map Room:
mcwetboy.net/maproom/

Mappery:
http://mappery.com

Museo del Ferrocarril, Madrid:
museodelferrocarril.org

National Library of Australia:
nla.gov.au

National Railway Museum, York:
—Picture Library: ssplprints.com/index.php

NASA:
—Image search: http://nix.nasa.gov/

Norman B. Leventhal Map Center at the Boston Public Library:
http://maps.bpl.org

Dmitry Parovoz's Russian and Baltic railway maps:
http://parovoz.com/indexe.php

Railserver:
railserve.com

Railroad.net forums:
railroad.net/forums

Railway Gazette International:
railwaygazette.com

Railways Through Europe:
bueker.net/trainspotting/maps.php

Railway Technology:
railway-technology.com

Rob Armstrong's Rail Industry Info pages:
rail-industry.info

Seat 61:
seat61.com

SkyscraperCity Forum:
—Railways: skyscrapercity.com/forumdisplay.php?f=812
—Rail maps: skyscrapercity.com/showthread.php?t=1042685

Strange Maps:
http://bigthink.com/blogs/strange-maps

UK National Archives/Public Record Office:
nationalarchives.gov.uk

University of Texas Perry-Castañeda Library Map Collection:
lib.utexas.edu/maps/map_sites/country_sites.html

Urban Rail:
urbanrail.net

Wikipedia:
http://en.wikipedia.org/wiki/Rail_transport_by_country
http://en.wikipedia.org/wiki/List_of_countries_by_rail_transport_network_size
http://en.wikipedia.org/wiki/List_of_national_archives

RAIL MUSEUMS

For a fuller list of rail museums and exhibitions around the world, check online (for example, http://en.wikipedia.org/wiki/Railway_Museum or http://www.wwfry.org/links.html), but here are some of those consulted by the author—opening hours, precise location and contact details of virtually all can be found with a simple Web search.

AFRICA
The Bulawayo Railway Museum, Raylton, Zimbabwe.
Egyptian National Railway Museum, Cairo, Egypt.
Nairobi Railway Museum, Nairobi, Kenya.
South African National Railway Museum, Johannesburg, SA.
Zambia Railway Museum, Livingstone, Zambia.

AMERICAs
California State Railroad Museum, Sacramento, California, USA.
Canadian Railway Museum Delson, Quebec, Canada.
Ferrocarril Interoceanico, Cuautla, Morelos, Mexico.
Midwest Central Railroad Museum, Iowa, USA.

National Railway Museum, Tacna, Peru.
New York Transit Museum, Brooklyn, NY, USA.

ASIA
Ambarawa Railway Museum, Central Java, Indonesia.
Beijing Railway Museum, North Road, Chaoyang, Beijing.
Darjeeling Himalayan Railway Museum, India.
Hejaz Railway Museum, Medina, Saudi Arabia.
Israel Railway Museum, Haifa, Israel.
Kotsu Kagaku Hakubutsukan, Osaka, Japan.
National Railway Museum, Chanakyapuri, New Delhi, India.
The Railway Museum, Saitama, near Tokyo, Japan

EUROPE
Budapest Museum of Transport, Hungary.
Central Museum of Railway Transport, St. Petersburg, Russia.
Crewe Heritage Centre, Crewe, Cheshire, UK.
Danmarks Jernbanemuseum, Odense, Denmark.

DB Museum, Nürnberg, Germany.
Glasgow Museum of Transport, UK.
Latvian Railway History Museum, Riga, Latvia.
London Transport Museum, Covent Garden, London, UK.
Museo del Ferrocarril, Atocha, Madrid, Spain.
Musée des Transports, Chelles, France
Musée Français du Chemin de Fer, Mulhouse, France.
National Railway Museum, York, UK.
Nederlands Spoorwegmuseum, Utrecht, Netherlands.
Richskaya Railway Museum, Moscow, USSR.
Suomen Rautatiemuseo, Hyvinkää, Finland.
Sveriges Järnvägsmuseum, Gävle, Gästrikland, Sweden.
Ulster Folk and Transport Museum, Cultra, Belfast, UK.

OCEANIA
MOTAT, Western Springs, Auckland, New Zealand.
National Railway Museum, Port Adelaide, South Australia.

INDEXES

GEOGRAPHIC

ABOVE: Cover of Mark's first book, Transit Maps of the World. *Now an international bestseller, it contains the official maps of all urban rail systems.* BELOW: Poster taken from Transit Maps of the World *designed by Mark.*

Author/London Transport Museum

BAGAGES

Author

ABOVE: Cover of Mark's second book. BELOW: Mark's map on a gift item.

London Transport Museum Shop

ABOUT THE AUTHOR
M A R K   O V E N D E N

CENTER: *The tiled/stone engraved map of Brittany rail services from the ticket hall of Dinard station, France, which Mark claims as his favorite surprise cartographic find of 2010.*

"Ovenden does what no other design history book has ever done"
Will Grimes, New York Times
on Mark Ovenden's Transit Maps of the World

FAR LOWER LEFT: *Mark after New York launch of* Transit Maps of the World, *in 2007*
BELOW: *Mark engrossed in papers for book research, summer 2004.*

Ivan Depetrovsky

Mark Ovenden, a Paris-based Englishman and Fellow of The Royal Geographical Society, specializes in books about rail cartography and transit design. A radio and TV producer and a journalist for many years, he, like most budding authors, contemplated his book concept for some time. After much research, his lifelong collection of transit maps became the basis of his first book (Metro Maps of the World), published in Britain in 2003. Encouraged by its success, Mark devoted his attention to writing full-time. It wasn't long before Penguin USA signed him up to produce an updated version of his book, published as Transit Maps of the World in 2007. It received critical acclaim and became an international bestseller.

Mark meantime relocated from London to Paris to focus on a new work about the Métro. His next Penguin book was Paris Underground: The Maps, Stations, and Design of the Metro. Still in the French capital he passionately claims, "The importance of design in promoting rail transit is undergoing a renaissance, which is good for riders, great for operators, and imperative for cutting pollution to protect our environment."

Rex Goddard